Awakening the Psychic Self

A CHRISTIAN PERSPECTIVE

Deanna Marie Riddick

REDFeather™

MIND | BODY | SPIRIT

4880 Lower Valley Road, Atglen, PA 19310

To my father

Cover design by Brenda McCullen
Type set in Tandelle, Schadow BT, Arial & Minion Pro

ISBN: 978-0-7643-5721-3
Printed in China

Published by Red Feather Mind, Body, Spirit
An imprint of Schiffer Publishing, Ltd.
4880 Lower Valley Road
Atglen, PA 19310
Phone: (610) 593-1777; Fax: (610) 593-2002
E-mail: Info@schifferbooks.com
Web: www.redfeatherpub.com

For our complete selection of fine books on this and related subjects, please visit our website at www.schifferbooks.com. You may also write for a free catalog.

Schiffer Publishing's titles are available at special discounts for bulk purchases for sales promotions or premiums. Special editions, including personalized covers, corporate imprints, and excerpts, can be created in large quantities for special needs. For more information, contact the publisher.

We are always looking for people to write books on new and related subjects. If you have an idea for a book, please contact us at proposals@schifferbooks.com.

Contents

A Note on God

I must address this dilemma of God, who or what it is, at the outset, since I reference "him" repeatedly throughout this book. I make no assumptions about the commonality of our definitions. Rather, I present to you an alternative exposition of this contested figure from otherworldly beings. What is God? Creative force. Love. Source energy. Divine thought. Divine mind. Wisdom. Holy mother-father. Goddess. All that is. Upon meeting my guides and angels, I questioned them about this enigmatic force we've come to call God. Without hesitation they explained to me simply that God is all that is. Prior to this angelic revelation, I purposefully had begun redirecting my prayers toward a "holy mother-father" God. I shifted my belief from a complete male deity to one that embodied both forms of energy. I thought I had made progress as I was transitioning from a Christian perception of God to a metaphysical one. But when it was unveiled to me that God is all that is, I couldn't quite comprehend the depth and magnitude of this truth.

Like many Christians, I believed that God embodied all of man's dynamic attributes. Of course this means I believed God to be man, or at least some kind of man wielding a sword of righteousness, judgment, and condemnation. The angelic version of what God IS wholeheartedly violated my ironclad interpretation. For my Christian self, this definition was far too transcendental, and I struggled to truly digest the spatial and energetic composition of all that is.

The angels presented me with an encyclopedic vision of the creative force that is God, which is unlimited by the physical and eternal in its love for all. This primary force encompasses all conceivable genders and elemental energy dispersed across the universe. The *all that is*, is eternal love, forgiveness, and total acceptance. This is an abstract and intangible definition of God, which makes him unreachable and perhaps even unrelatable. For most, it is an uncomfortable perception and it disrupts the foundations of our normative ideas of a corporeal entity. I fully support this abstraction of God and embrace this alternative definition. While this is my understanding of God, and the God I reference in this book, I will continue to refer to God as "him."

PART I

Christian Conflicts and Psychic Revelations

Introduction

Psychic is a dirty word. It evokes feelings of suspicion, distrust, and skepticism among the general public, and this is not without cause. Unfortunately, pseudo psychics have masqueraded as initiates of the divine for centuries and have capitalized on the sorrows and desperation of true seekers. This idea of the pseudo psychic continues to gain ground in mainstream society. Because of this, true psychics have suffered a particular social stigma and are commonly ostracized in the public eye; therefore, their practices are no longer considered holy and sacred. From a Christian mindset, "supernatural powers," such as prophecy or clairvoyance, are bestowed only to those who conform to the rules and laws of a Christian god. Additionally, Christian laws forbid the pursuit of divine help in the company of a psychic and beyond the sanctity of the church.

Broadly speaking, Christians take a pledge of understanding that only sanctified priests, cardinals, ministers, bishops, and preachers, who live according to God's laws, have access to divine wisdom and knowledge, as well as God's ear. It is only they who can earn the gifts of God and his favor since they are the only beings qualified to speak to God and act as intermediaries between Heaven and Earth. This has set an unfortunate precedent for arbiters of the psychic ministry. Without an affiliation to a religious institution, and without the brand of legitimization from a church, psychics suffer allegations of fraudulence and thievery, as well as accusations of witchcraft and Devil worship. How do psychics prove that they, too, perform God's work, which is condoned by God and has an appropriate place here in this world? How do we move beyond the confines of this stifled system of religious thought and shift into an inclusive and comprehensive narrative that challenges enduring perceptions of psychics?

First, we must seek to remember our collective identity as spirits, rather than to pit psychic against Christian. As it stands, a majority of us ground our identity in the three-dimensional plane. This means that we define ourselves according to our relationship to the body and to our Earthly titles and social status and their associated meanings and values. The fabric of our identity is detrimentally shaped by our comparisons to others physically, socially, economically, politically, and even spiritually. The evaluation of our spiritual identity is based on the depth of our commitment to the church. Spiritual primacy and a godlike identity are bestowed upon those who publicly bear the order of the cloth and occupy a religious title that distinguishes them from the general masses. It is at this juncture of categorical divisiveness where we experience a mass crisis of identity.

We are not defined by our choice whether or not to attend church, or even if we decide to devote our professional lives to the church or a religious conclave. Our identity has already been established prior to our physical incarnation. As iterated in the Bible, we, meaning every living being and consciousness, are made in the image of God. Simply put, we are bearers of the rays of God's light, which include the attributes of unconditional love, forgiveness, compassion, patience, wisdom, knowledge, and even spiritual gifts. As such, we are eternally connected to God. There is no separation between God and man, and the sun and its rays. This knowledge has crucial implications for how we perceive our identity. If we all are created of the substance of all things God and are eternally connected to God, then we all are godlike. This eschews the necessity of a special human intermediary for godly interpretation and communion. This means that we all are equally divine, whether we are of the cloth or sanctified by the churches of the Earth. For many Christians, it is blasphemous to believe and accept that we all are equally divine. During our Earthly incarnation, we are taught to subscribe to titles that distinguish us, and the formation of these titles relies upon practicing judgment based solely on our personal and collective values and beliefs. Although one of the prime tenets of Christianity is not to judge others, it becomes second nature to evaluate and appraise according to the laws of this religion. Christian churches contain a hierarchal makeup with levels of distinction based on spiritual magnitude. In Catholicism, the pope is the head of the church and has been deemed God's representative on Earth. It is difficult to believe that we are equally divine in the eyes of God when one person is attributed the title of the Lord's spokesperson. During church service, we are made keenly aware of our inherently sinful nature at birth and are told to repent in the hopes that God will grant mercy on our soul. This message implies a strong separation from God and our godlike nature. It diminishes our self-worth and supports beliefs about our limited potential. It is at this juncture where psychic work makes the most impact. Psychics are a part of the soul community that brings forth positive and divine messages professing our eternal unification with God, and they divulge the truth about the equality of our holiness. Additionally, they are a reflection of the truism that each and every one possesses the gifts of spirit, including clairvoyance, clairaudience, and clairsentience. Per God, a gift given to one is a gift given to all. Ask and you shall receive because God denies us not. Regardless of the mistakes we have made, we all are spiritual channels of the divine and endowed with celestial gifts. God can work through us only while we live here on Earth, and he chooses through which medium we may be of spiritual service.

Second, we must truly redefine the ministry of the psychic in an effort to dismantle the erroneous consciousness surrounding the nature of their work. There is an unfortunate collective misunderstanding of the psychic, whereby they are endowed with special mystical powers unexplained by "natural laws" operating in opposition to the natural order of God's doctrine. The Greek word *psychic* means "to be of the soul." To be psychic is to exist in your natural state of being without any limitations. Psychics consciously operate as spiritual conduits who allow the power of God's cosmic energy, knowledge, and unlimited potential, to be transmitted through them. Psychics openly maintain their cosmic channel to the divine and engage in celestial communion. They freely accept the gifts of God, which include telepathy, clairvoyance, clairaudience, clairsentience, healing, channeling, prophecy, mediumship, and even speaking in tongues. These gifts of the soul are innate in all beings. No one is specially selected to be endowed with these "powers." All are naturally endowed. Your rejection of these gifts does not negate their presence or their power. So, what constitutes the ministry of the psychic?

The ministry of the psychic in no way differs from those who reject the notion of the soul. All are here to be of service to one another and to offer love, which is the immaculacy of God's work. However, what does differ here is the form in which the service is performed. Psychics openly acknowledge their God-given gifts and utilize their developed skills to connect to guides and angels and other light beings to help people solve problems, redirect systems of thought, connect to the deceased to heal wounds, help people remember their divinity, and demonstrate that life is eternal through mediumship. The information that is accessed is objective and loving if it is truly coming from the celestial realms. Psychics are simply holy messengers. Within their messages lies knowledge of the spiritual laws of love and justice, emanating from God, which order and structure the universe.

This ministry also brings to the fore our true holy parentage. We have within our very own spiritual design the natural ability to commune and engage in holy dialogue with our Heavenly mother/father. God transmits knowledge to us all to help us learn, heal, and grow. Like a parent to their child, this information is given from God with love to his children, that being us. Psychics, or holy messengers, are reflective of this type of relationship between God, the eternal mother-father, and his-her children, or the children of the Earth. Please note that we all are holy messengers; however, this is clearly seen in the ministry of the psychic, which is the ministry of love and demonstration. Psychics openly affirm their role as a child of God and publicly acknowledge their holy gifts through the art of performance. By being of service and employing their gifts, they show the eternal sacred connection between themselves and God.

Psychic ministry is devoted to bringing forth knowledge that empowers the masses. Such knowledge includes the principles of our divine parentage and selfhood. What can be more powerful? As we seek to individually and collectively understand the source of our identity, the pillars of truth will be revealed before us. And this is that all are holy divine creations of God. With this knowledge before us, we possess the ability to dispel long-standing myths about our separation from God and the concept of the divine. We are the spiritual kinfolk of God, separated temporarily only by birth in the three-dimensional plane, but never in spirit or in truth. In the psychic ministry, this is a truism. And psychics rely on the divine umbilical cord wherein the Heavenly father/mother is always available to spiritually nourish and teach and heal.

Again, this ministry requires challenging and reinterpreting antiquated definitions of the divine. The term *divine* is historically synonymous with a clergyman, theologian, and priest. However, this ministry advocates a shift in focus toward our biospiritual relationship with God, the collective father/mother. By doing so, we will see that our actual spiritual DNA mirrors that of our spiritual parent, which is divine in design. This title of divinity is not segregated to one sector of society. It belongs to everyone. I am not advocating a dismissal of religious emissaries in the church, since God speaks and works through everyone. Rather, I am proposing here a radical acceptance of our true godly and psychic nature.

The development of the psychic self is simply a call to awaken and remember who we really are. By actively seeking and learning these truths about our identity and applying them, we facilitate the transformation of the soul—this is the journey of the psychic.

The first part of *Awakening* tells the story of the unfoldment of my true divine self. I spent my adolescent and early adult years as a fearful and negative-thinking Christian. My mind was a haven for all thoughts of God the punisher, Jesus the savior, and Satan the evil doer. At no point in time did I question the truism that was my innate sinful nature. Concurrently, I secretly carried the burden of hearing whispers in the halls and bedrooms of our house, calling out to me. I spent years endlessly fraught with terror from the unseen realms. In the kitchen, bathroom, bedroom, and dining room, I heard spirits call to me. My nights were filled with prayers as I begged God to deliver me from evil, to save me and protect me from the Devil. While in the church pews, I bent down on my knees and quietly bargained with God, promising to behave if he would just save me. But the voices continued to find their way to me.

This experience was quite a lonely one. I could not share it with my parents or my sisters. I agonized over the religious battle between good and evil and panicked that I was on the losing side. As a compulsive Christian, I read the book of Revelation to prepare myself for Armageddon. Hysterically I tried to ready myself to be on the winning side. As a teenager, I had a spiritually uncultivated mind and was sadly unaware that this battle was an internal one. With the help of my father and the failure to be "saved" by Jesus Christ, I began to seek an alternative route. I struggled to find anyone in church who spoke of being chased by disembodied entities. I had yet to locate anyone who could reconcile the messages of the Bible with my personal experiences of hearing voices. My spirit compelled me to look beyond Christianity for answers. Herein lies the struggle at the beginning of this journey. To seek for truth within self, beyond the comforting familiarity of Christianity, and even reclaim our psychic self is no easy feat, especially for those who have already invested their faith in a particular belief system. Christian guilt can be incredibly powerful, since we feel we have committed spiritual treason and abandoned God if we seek understanding outside the church. As I began my sacred expedition, I questioned everything. I interrogated the reality of the psychic realm, including the legitimate existence of spirit guides, angels, and archangels. As I developed, I challenged my clairvoyant visions, disembodied voices, and any psychic reading I received. I was certain of God's impending wrath but persevered nonetheless. I experienced many emotional mutinies as I shifted away from the Christian definition of God and the belief of unholy psychics. I felt the crushing weight of guilt as I departed from Christian scripture and read literature by psychics and mediums. However, I felt a sense of relief when I came across people who had been experiencing the exact same phenomenon. It took many years to reconcile my beliefs with Christianity and to put my full faith in God throughout my search.

I learned that God's guidance manifests in the form of intuition, a knowingness. For all, we hear this as an inner voice. And for me, in particular, it came from my higher self, the inner voice, angels, archangels, and my spirit guide. When I decided to open my heart to God, my gifts flourished and with that came some understanding. This mighty pilgrimage propelled me through cycles of Christian guilt, forgiveness, doubt, fear manifested in varied forms, and rhapsodies of joy, gratitude, and love. You will see in this book that I rectified many spiritual dilemmas by bridging biblical scriptures and teachings with psychic work and by identifying powerful psychics in the Bible whose work was condoned by God. Throughout my pursuit of the truth, I met my spirit guides, guardian angels, archangels, and many other entities who stepped forward to guide me and expound some very fundamental and enlightening principles. These principles presented in this book helped me navigate unchartered spiritual territories and bury restrictive and injurious religious beliefs.

The quest of the psychic is one of trust and mental expansion. It requires first and foremost that you allow and trust your intuition to guide you. To intuit is to know or receive (or both) by intuition, allowing your spirit to take the reins of your mind. While you are reclaiming and developing your psychic gifts, and intuiting, you may receive guidance that is in complete opposition to your expectations and your beliefs, contradictory to scripture, and seemingly illogical. Even if the advice is helpful, uplifting, loving, and supportive, you may doubt and choose to ignore it. This is why psychics must be willing to expand their mind, meaning that they accept and trust new knowledge straight from the divine source. Your intuition will naturally perform as your tool of discernment. God will directly lead you to people and books to teach you and support your path, and you will be met with validation every step of the way. The secret in the sauce is belief and faith. Please note that my objective is not to force you to abandon your beliefs. Rather, I am emphasizing the necessity for more faith in God and yourself.

One of the goals of this book was to unveil, through my personal journey, how I learned the truth about who we are. My intention is not to force people to give up their day jobs to "become a psychic." Rather, my hope is to promote the knowledge that you already are. You have been given a power that is within you, but not of you. All are gifted with a mode of communion with the creator beyond the five senses. These modalities include spiritual sight, sound, and feeling of energy. My hope is that you are brave enough to trust God's guidance and accept what is preinstalled within your being. For practicing Christians struggling with their gifts, I truly hope that my journey will demonstrate the fact that these gifts are natural, not evil or supernatural. I truly encourage you to follow your heart because therein lies the truth of God; he will lead you on your path. I am hopeful that this book will comfort you during your own spiritual pilgrimage.

Awakening the Psychic Self

The objective of the second part of this book is to teach you how to awaken your dormant spiritual abilities. It comprises metaphysical exercises that will help you learn and develop your natural psychic gifts, including clairvoyance, clairaudience, and clairsentience. For newcomers, and for those already on this path, I hope that the information and exercises included here will expand your gifts and your relationship with the creator force or your higher power. The techniques provided in this book were shown and taught to me from my guides and angels for the development of my gifts, and it is my hope that they will initiate the progression and strengthening of yours.

CHAPTER 1

Christian Beginnings

THIS STORY DOES not begin with the adolescent nurturing of my spiritual development. My parents knew nothing about New Age phenomena, metaphysics, spirit guides, or listening to your intuition, and no one spoke about angels in our household. There wasn't some guru who just happened to find me and tell me that I was the chosen one. What you'll find here is my truth, as ugly and messy and liberating as it can be.

I guess you can say my journey began like everyone else's—with hesitancy, fear, lack of trust, guilt, and doubt. To be clear, I was raised a Christian. As an adolescent I attended church on Friday nights and on Sunday, and I sang in the church choir. I have even been baptized twice. I played Mother Mary in the Christmas play, as well as the messenger archangel Gabriel, when I could get the part. Church was a fun social forum for my younger self.

My father was a military man, and my older sister, Nicole, and I spent our early youth traveling the States until my parent's divorce and my father's marriage to his second wife. My stepmother had a daughter, Beatrice, whom we quickly befriended. We moved from the open plains of Cheyenne, Wyoming, to Athens, Greece, for six years, where my parents had another daughter, Casey. Two years after her birth, we moved to San Antonio, Texas. Shortly thereafter, my stepmother's mother moved from Maryland into our new Texas home.

My step-grandmother was a bona fide minister, and she let everyone know it. She was a short, chubby woman with dirty-brown eyes, and her skin was colored a rich and creamy ebony. She wore thick, metal-framed glasses and a resting stern look across her face. She was a bit too serious for my taste. The chaffing of her pantyhose always signaled her entrance into the room. I knew at that time that she didn't much care for my sister and me, but I did learn two things from her: "Don't put a question mark where God has put a period," and "In order to go to Heaven you have to be saved."

Now, I'll admit, at thirteen years old I didn't have the slightest clue as to what it meant to be "saved." Saved from what, exactly? And from whom? All I knew was that I had to have it. Being saved, that is, so that my soul wouldn't be condemned to eternal Hellfire and brimstone. From my understanding, Satan was a true entity who lived and breathed. He definitely had a pitchfork and a host of minions to do his bidding. Church informed me that Satan was indeed a fallen angel whose end goal was to misguide all of humanity and trap us. My grandmother reminded me to be on alert, because Satan and his host of demons were ever present. Just the talk of demons scared me straight. I believed in possession and all methods, or scare tactics, employed by all of his minions. I felt that I had a good understanding of Satan and his Earthly mission.

My parents were not devout Christians. They did their fair share of drinking and partying, but they were believers. My father was a deacon at the church we attended, and my sisters and I sang in the very small church choir. The church we attended was white with a small steeple. It was called Emmanuel Apostolic. This little church had weathered many Texas-sized storms, and the paint was chipping off the sides of the building. Ten rows of pews lined the creaky hardwood floors. In the front of the church was a wooden podium, a small drum set, and an old, dusty Casio keyboard. There were no windows, and the lights were dim and yellow; the air was always thick and serious. This little church held about fifteen congregates in total. There was no room to hide if you fell asleep or if you received a slap or spanking for acting up. Every Sunday an elderly black woman with short, black, curly hair and thin bangs sat in the pool pit clapping her hands and catching flies in the church. Another woman wailed about how the Devil was trying to keep her down. Every Sunday the pastor sermonized about descending into a Hellish afterlife where our souls encompassed eternal thirst, desiring water but finding none because we all were sinners. He counseled the congregates that Jesus was coming back for only one church, and it needed to be *this* church, so we had to get our house in order for the arrival of Christ. He reminded us that if we were saved, we would go to the land of milk and honey and be kings and queens in Heaven.

At the tender age of thirteen, after one Sunday service, my stepmother chided my older sister, Nicole, and me about making testimonies in church. She reminded us about suffering the weighted anger and displeasure of the Lord God. Testimony? I panicked. During the early-morning service at church, each member stood up behind the pews and made a statement expressing their extreme gratitude to Jesus for providing the means to pay a bill or put food on the table. Some testimonies were short or overly dramatized, resulting in wailing, clapping, and jumping. I wasn't quite certain I understood the holy business of testifying. Was this an act of gratitude? A confessional open mic? Nicole and I exchanged wide-eyed looks as we sat in the back of my stepmom's blue Nissan Sentra.

Of course I made it. I firmly stood up from the church pews and thanked the Lord for my dad's new car because his old one was an overheated piece of crap. I hoped this pleased the Lord, but surely, I had no way of knowing. A few church members laughed and some clapped, yelling, "Praise Jesus." I assumed I'd passed the test. From then on, I made a testimony at each church service to secure my mansion in Heaven. I thought to myself that I was a good Christian. I prayed at every meal and on my knees at bedtime. Every night, I submitted the following Child's Bedtime Prayer to Heaven above: "Now I lay me, down to sleep, I pray the Lord my soul to keep, if I shall die, before I wake, I pray the Lord my soul to take."[1] I was raised to believe that there was a god up there somewhere in the blue sky resting on the clouds ready to send me to Hell if I screwed up.

My step-grandmother's bedroom was next to mine on the second floor of our house. She spent her evenings squinting her eyes reading her Bible and watching westerns on a small, wooden box TV with a large, crooked antenna. One day I approached my step-grandmother and asked her how I could go about getting saved. She pointed her index finger to the light-brown carpet floor and clearly instructed me to get on my knees and repeat, "Thank you, Jesus," en rote until I was saved. And, of course, I did as I was told. I got on my knees and began to repeat myself over and over, but to my dismay, nothing happened. Nicole came to watch and sat on the bed next to my step-grandmother. I can't remember exactly how long I kneeled, but what I can remember is that my knees were beginning to ache and burn on the carpet, so I quit. I slowly raised my eyes to her, and she told me we could try again later. I wondered, What was I doing wrong? This was the first of many failed attempts.

Every few months or so, our small church would hold a "revival." Revivals are Christian church services, mainly held in the South, whose aim is to restore or renew one's relationship with God. Some services are aimed at gaining new converts, but at our church, the goal was to be baptized and saved by the end of the service. These usually occurred late on Sunday mornings and nights, which Nicole and I dreaded because we knew we would have to be at church from sunup to sundown.

During revival, the pastor explained the importance of baptism and being saved by Jesus. I always wondered, as I still do now, how does one demonstrate that Jesus has officially saved them? How does one know? In my church, people demonstrated their holiness and obtainment of the Holy Ghost by dancing up and down the aisles and speaking in tongues. I witnessed many church congregants run and jump and scream, *Hallelujah Jesus*! Some clapped their hands and jumped simultaneously. Others just skipped and screamed while their church dresses swayed wildly across their bodies. Occasionally some members expressed great physical agility and moved like James Brown in between the pews. In our church, one also exhibited they were saved by speaking in tongues. Speaking in tongues is a phenomenon where the "saved" speak in God's language. It was always unclear to me whether the person receiving this message directly from God actually understood the message. But, what I did know was that if you could demonstrate speaking in tongues, then you were certifiably saved. If you were "filled with the Holy Ghost," you were saved. And everyone knew it.

As a very young teenager I was determined to get saved. I heard about the end of days in church, and I feared the worst. Church members often spoke of Jesus's return to Earth. When was Jesus coming back and why? What was the second coming supposed to look like, and would I be prepared? During the winter months in Texas, there were stormy days filled with golf ball–sized hail, and I was sure that the four horsemen of the apocalypse were near. I prayed even more on those nights, asking that God save me from the impending rapture.

During every Sunday service at church, my pastor requested that unsaved souls walk up to the altar to receive the Holy Ghost. Again, at fifteen, I was determined. I failed many times before, and I could not fathom burning in

Hell or in the lake of fire for all of eternity. Some nights I lay on my bed trying to imagine what it would be like to physically burn. How long *would* we actually burn? Did it feel like a thousand suns burning through my flesh and bones? Would I feel my skin slowly melt? What an awful way to suffer for true eternity. In my mind, God was most certainly cruel and perhaps a bit of a sadomasochist.

I slowly walked up to the altar and waited behind two other people. I was surprised that Nicole did not follow me. Didn't she know what was coming? As I stood in line I turned my head back to look at her; she shook her head no. Our pastor was a short, elderly, bald man. He used his cane to stand up and reached for the bottle of castor oil sitting on a nearby stool. For those unaware, in many Christian churches, oil is commonly used to anoint an individual. My pastor dabbed a few drops onto his fingers and rubbed an oily cross onto my forehead. I closed my eyes, hoping that God would take pity on me and finally save my soul. The pastor laid his hand on my head, while another woman prayed over me. She was hollering. Shouting, really. Her raspy voice echoed throughout my right ear canal. She asked the Lord Jesus to save my soul. I waited and waited and waited. And as I waited, the pastor yelled *Hallelujah* and slammed his oily hand against my forehead and knocked me to the ground. In shock, I lay there with my eyes closed, hoping for some sort of transformation. I witnessed on many occasions people filled with the Holy Ghost, and I was prepared for its possession. I lay there imagining the power of this energy coursing through my veins, forcing me to sit up and jump and perhaps speak in a new language, our holy mother tongue. I lay there giving permission to the Holy Ghost to use me. After a few minutes, I wondered if I was supposed to move? How long was I supposed to lie there? The pastor clapped and thanked Jesus for saving me. I looked around the church, hoping to be blessed with a new set of eyes, but I felt the same. I stood up and walked back to the pews to sit with my sister and mother. Insatiably curious, they both asked me how it felt. Did I feel different? What did I see? Was I transformed and finally saved by Jesus? I responded that the pastor slammed me to the ground and I felt nothing but a lump on the back of my head. My mother and sister began to giggle like a company of schoolgirls, but I did not laugh. This was holy business. Why didn't Jesus want to save me?

My family moved when I was fifteen to Austin, Texas. We no longer attended church, but I still prayed twice a day and at breakfast and dinner. I can say that at this time in my life, at the ripe old age of fifteen, I was very afraid of God, Hell, and, of course, death. I was sure that my life would end with harsh judgment from God and a cast-iron stairway to Hell.

My fears even seeped into my dreams. During the day I was discussing *Lord of the Flies* in my English class, and by night I had nightmares about the last judgment. These nightmares always ended with me standing in a short line into Heaven's gates or in an incredibly long line with an arrow pointing down on an engraved placard reading, "Hell, this way." It was frightening, but I was relieved to be told I was in the wrong line and I belonged in Heaven. Sometimes.

CHAPTER 2

Voices

I STRUGGLE TO remember the details of my entire childhood; there are only glimpses of tire swings, Barbie® dolls, and playing cards. I can, however, remember the wispy voices lining the dark corners of my room and the exasperated cries for attention lingering beside my bed. I cannot say when this began exactly, or even when I first noticed it. I recollect being terrified of the dark, and I hated sleeping by myself. I was always certain that something was hovering over me, watching me and coming to get me in the middle of the night.

While in high school I prayed at night for Jesus to protect me. I learned during many church services there were demons here on this planet who wanted to possess us and take our souls. And I was a straight believer. In the spectrum of my Christian mind, demons were real, and I knew for sure they were haunting me and coming to kidnap me at night.

During those years, I developed a bedtime ritual to protect myself against all things evil. My blankets and sheets became my protective barriers against Satan and his demons. I pulled them over my head and buried my face in my pillow, hoping that if I closed my eyes, they wouldn't exist or would at least disappear. These voices were a recurring act during my high school years. In the middle of the night, after drifting into deep sleep, whispers pierced through the silence, calling my name, "Dena." Dena is my nickname, and only my family knows me by this name. In the beginning, I thought my sisters were playing a prank on me, but they were fast asleep. As a source of comfort, I tried to ignore the initial whispers by telling myself I was dreaming. As I slept through the night, the voices gradually became louder and louder, affirming my name, "Dena." My first response was to call on Jesus for protection. Although he rejected saving me at church, I was hopeful he would protect me in my time of need. I never dared raise my face from underneath the sheets to see if anyone was in the room, and I definitely never asked who was there. My best policy was to ignore it, pretend that I did not hear it, and assume it would go away. But every night it was the same. "Dena." And I could tell no one. During high school, I heard raspy voices reaching for me from the ethers. These voices were not gender specific. I had no way of discerning whether they were distinctively female or male, young or old.

I wondered if anyone else was experiencing this type of phenomenon, but I never asked. And I never shared these experiences either. My parents were divorced and my mother was not in my life. I lacked a mother-daughter connection with my stepmother, and my father had his own internal demons he was battling. Our house was a quiet one where rules were obeyed without question. There was a lack of love and affection, and no one really spoke to each other much. I always followed a majority of the rules. I never sneaked out of the house, and I never attended any parties. I never tried drugs or drank alcohol. I was afraid of my parents, and I always kept to myself, writing every chance I could.

I feared every night that demons were coming for me. My step-grandmother told me that demons were short, black figures, who sometimes wore capes. I heard them call my name as a whisper and sometimes as a short and choppy shout. Without doubt they were definitely trying to garner my attention. At times throughout my youth, I shared a room with one or two of my sisters, but that did not dissuade the voices from trying to capture my attention. In their traditional fashion, they woke me up in the middle of the night, calling my name in shaky, nettling whispers.

When I was young, my parents rented scary movies for my sisters and me to watch when they planned to leave the house for an evening party. The characters from those films always followed me into my dreams. My nightmares took me to the occasional boiler room, hiding from a scary man with a burnt face. I often woke up profusely sweating with heart palpitations, afraid for my life. At that time, I did not realize how watching those films could affect my psyche and even my own reality. It was because of those films, and my weekly religious dose of Hellfire and brimstone, that I believed dark entities were trying to possess me or, at the very least, hurt me or trick me.

I'm sure you're wondering why I never asked who was calling my name or why they were there. This is somewhat difficult to explain. Part of me feared that if I responded, it would open some sort of gateway to Hell, and I definitely did not want that. I suppose that the other part of me thought that I was perhaps schizophrenic at some level. I was confused and utterly frightened. I never answered. Not even once.

I never saw a ghost, figures, or shadow people, but I could hear something cry my name almost every night. I never bothered to tell anyone, nor did I bother to research what was happening to me. After all, I was young and had other priorities. But I always knew what to expect when night fell.

At the age of fifteen, I had an unusual experience with a disembodied voice. One particular evening, my sister's boyfriend came to our house to watch a movie after my parents had gone to bed. I went to sleep early that night and slept with the lights off, which was completely unusual, so I must have been exhausted. About three hours into my sleep, I heard a thundering voice and felt the house shake off its foundation. "Dena!" My name echoed throughout the entire house. I was certain my entire family was awake and running to my aid. Immediately I jumped up from my bed, my knees shaking, and replied, "Yes, yes," panting heavily. My eyes darted around in the darkness. The voice was not human, and it carried the vocal weight of 10,000 men. I didn't know where it came from or who it was or how they managed to be in my bedroom, but they were there and wanted their presence known. There was no response from the voice.

I sprinted down the carpeted stairs and didn't even bother to check if I was dressed. I ended up in the living room, where my sister was sitting alone on the couch in front of the TV, waiting for her boyfriend to come out of the bathroom. Breathing heavily, I asked her, "Did you hear that?" I could barely catch my breath. "Hear what?" she replied. "Did you hear that voice call me?" She looked at me confused and said, "No." No one in the house was awake except my sister, her boyfriend, and me. No one came to help me at all because no one else had heard it. Needless to say, I did not sleep the rest of the night.

At this juncture I truly believed that Satan's minions were determined to capture me, possess my soul, take over my body, and spin my head. I thought that I was an awful sinner. A true textbook sinner. Legions of fearful thoughts penetrated my every being. What had I done to offend God? Why did Satan want me so badly? What sins had I committed that Hell wanted me now?

I never told my step-grandmother about these occurrences even though she was a minister. I knew she would tell me they were demons and bless me with anointed canola oil. Of course I knew she would tell me to pray, which I was already doing without any evidence of success. I definitely did not want my mother or father to know, for fear of laughter or institutionalization. I never even told a pastor or religious figure about my experiences. I just accepted my fate.

It was against God to seek beyond the church for answers, so I refrained from doing so. I cannot say that I wasn't curious. I had never been taken to an actual psychic or had my palms read. The Bible and television were my only frame of reference for what a psychic actually did and what their practice entailed. My church taught me that psychics, mystics, and fortune tellers were an abomination, and as such, they would be punished by God.

My belief in this law was tested at my new high school in Austin, where I met a fair-haired girl, who wasn't necessarily a mystic or a psychic, but she was into what I deemed "other things," or anything outside the church. She invited me to go with her and her mother to a palm reader one Saturday, and I eagerly said yes. Even though I knew it was against God, and it would only increase my potential for crossing the boundary into Hell, I went anyway. We arrived at a small bookstore that smelled of sage and nag champa incense and was lined with druid robes and other ritual paraphernalia. In truth, I cannot remember what she said that day, with the exception that my life would be short. There was no mention of hearing voices or Satan or the like. I was secretly hoping that this woman would see something about me and identify the truth behind my experiences. Needless to say, I was not happy to hear her message, so I completely dismissed it.

I never really sought out psychics, mediums, healers, or teachers after high school. But I did seek answers during my early college years. I read many books about near-death experiences that preached Jesus was the only way to Heaven and that Hell was guaranteed for the population at large. Although fearful, I continued to read this literature, which only solidified my fear of God. I somehow managed to find myself around others who were seeking as I had been. Throughout my many jobs, there was someone actively reading similar literature who was just as convinced as I was that God was angry, jealous, and vengeful;

we learned it was wise not to cross him, or suffer the fate of burning flesh in the eternal lake of fire.

The voices continued throughout my twenties and early thirties while I was in graduate school. They spoke, but I remained too fearful to respond. They repeatedly called my name two to three times at night, and I ignored it or prayed for it to go away. I no longer attended church, and my dreams of Heaven and Hell disappeared altogether. I stopped reading books that discussed the afterlife; I felt that I had a pretty good grasp of what was in store for my soul, and I wanted to try to enjoy my life while I could. It wasn't until my early thirties that I would learn that it was a common phenomenon among mediums to hear voices throughout their youth.

CHAPTER 3

Minor Awakenings

I spent seven arduous years in graduate school, and toward the end of it I was miserable, alone, and depressed. I regretted being in the program and was constantly criticized; whatever semblance of confidence I had was completely destroyed. I needed help. My grant writing and project proposals were never good enough to secure any major fellowships. I spent all day, every day, at school studying, writing, teaching, and grading. My life felt meaningless and boring, and I often wondered what I was really contributing to the world. I constantly competed to prove myself to this institution and to my colleagues, and my enthusiasm was altogether gone. I needed a miracle to save me.

During the last three years of graduate school I began to seek a new way out. I lacked motivation and lost interest in the work I was doing. I held a grudge against the people I had to serve every day, and I filled my mind with fantasies of walking away from my degree. I was tired, but restless. I knew there was something greater, but I really did not know how to find it or even where to begin to look. My relationship with God was not as strong as it had previously been, but I knew that I needed him now more than ever. I no longer prayed nearly as much as I used to, and I was so absorbed in graduate school that it became my new religion. In truth, I had no desire to return to church. I did not want anyone to "lay hands" on me, nor did I want to be baptized for the third time. It was clear to me that getting saved was going to be difficult, and I wasn't sure that I ever *would* be saved. In my heart, I was beginning to feel that I should be enough for God, and I did not want, or need, anyone to speak to him on my behalf. I wanted a direct line and was willing to explore new territory to find it.

It must have been on television where I heard about meditation, but I assumed it was only for practicing Buddhists. On daytime talk shows I watched as enthusiastic guests professed the magic that is meditation. Recent converts reported experiencing mental states of serenity, peace, and euphoria all because of stilling the unruly mind. I wondered if that was just a Western fad. However, there must have been a reason for its expanding popularity, I thought, and it was worth a try. I was desperate at the time and needed something to save me from this vicious cycle I'd placed myself in. I was dissatisfied with school, I disliked what type of life I had created for myself, and I was ready to walk down a new path.

Like most, I did not have a guru to guide me. Exhausted from my own little world, I simply sat down one day on my living-room floor and closed my eyes. I asked God about meditation. What was meditation, and what was I supposed to expect? An awakening? Was I to await the arrival of some life-changing epiphany? Did meditation open new doors? I basically asked God to prove to me that there was truly another way. An alternative way to see, hear, think, and feel. I cannot say that I didn't feel the slight burden of Christian guilt that engulfed my psyche and enslaved my soul. There was a frightening possibility that God would frown upon this; after all, it wasn't the Christian way. I was taught that there was only one way to God and only one book to light the lamp. In complete disregard and pure desperation, I sat with my eyes closed on the linoleum floor and patiently waited. I saw nothing, nor did I hear a word about me. I sat in silence, just waiting for the universe to appear. And it did in the most unsuspecting way.

In retrospect, what I saw was purely an act of grace. I asked the divine creator to prove himself to me. Essentially, I tried to provoke him by saying, "Show me what you got." I admit I didn't feel the least bit arrogant, nor was I concerned if God were to strike me dead. After all, I believed I was a good girl. I didn't party, I didn't drink, I still came home at a reasonable hour. I was good on all fronts, I thought.

As I sat quietly on the floor, I felt my shoulders loosen and a wave of pressure settle over my head like thick fog rolling in over a mountain. Within ten minutes, I felt a thick-curtained veil pull away from face, and a reel of Polaroid* pictures quickly cycled across my view. Slowly, each photo appeared clearly within view and then retracted. I cannot remember the first few photos, but the last three told a story. In this vision, it was me, but it wasn't me. I stood in a room with my sister, wearing this god-awful faded orange dress with big purple flower print. I was pregnant, maybe around eight months. When the picture faded from my view, another one appeared. I saw a woman in a hospital bed sitting up holding a baby. I sat on the cold floor, holding this image in my mind, staring intently at the woman holding the baby. It took two minutes to realize that it was *me* in that hospital holding a baby. Was it mine? Shocked, I snapped out of my meditation.

Initially, I doubted my vision. I was under the impression that my being was to be infused with some otherworldly state of tranquility. What were these visions? I had difficulty differentiating between my imagination and the truth. Was I making this up? However, I truly could not deny that I did in fact see *something* that day. I was undeniably suspicious, skeptical, nervous, and intrigued. I had asked God to open a new way for me—was this it? Was this the true purpose of meditation? Was this the explanation for all the rave? In an attempt to make sense of what I was seeing and experiencing, I referenced the only book I knew that mentioned visions, the Bible. I knew that God provided messages to prophets through spiritual sight; was this happening to me? Who was I even to be *thinking* this? I was disgusted by my own spiritual arrogance. It was not only the visions themselves that startled me, but the content. The content of these visions provoked a series of questions. First, what was I really seeing, and why? Was this a trick of the mind or of the Devil? Moreover, *why* did I need to see this? These visions further forced me to question theories about having a predetermined life versus having free will. Are our lives already predetermined?

Still fascinated by what I saw and how I saw it, I knew I was going to meditate again. I thought that if I sat in the same place, the same way, I would again see the same thing or even something better. The next day I tried again. I closed my eyes with many ridiculous expectations. Initially everything was black. I waited patiently for some mystical magic to emerge from the ethers. In the same fashion as before, an uncomfortable, dense pressure settled over my head and pictures rapidly flew in and out of my view. It was as if I were ten years old again, and a friend was playing flashcards with me. None of the photos were recognizable at first; they were moving too fast. As they slowed down, I was able to see an old picture of a boy with his mother during a ski trip. Judging by the hairstyle, it must have been late 1980s, early 1990s. I just sat and focused on the details of the image. *Why am I seeing this?* I thought. I definitely did not recognize the boy or his mother and couldn't comprehend the reasoning behind this vision. I opened my mouth to tell them, or him, or whoever it was, that I got the picture, but what was it for?

As a general reminder, I knew nothing about the actual practice of meditation; I was oblivious about the process of opening and stilling my mind. Prior to this, I never focused on any sort of spiritual practice beyond the realm of Christianity. As I mentioned earlier, it was sinful to even delve into the world of other mystical practices. I had no knowledge about clairvoyance, clairaudience, clairsentience, or what I know now to be the gifts of the Creator.

Unexpectedly, I heard a voice rise from the ethers. It was a young boy's voice and it was hoarse, as if he was speaking in desperation, or trying to grasp for air. He responded, "Dead." At the start, I couldn't understand and asked him to repeat again. He responded, "Dead." I nodded and paused for a breath. There was a calm familiarity about this type of conversation. He proceeded to tell me about himself, little words slipping out here and there. The message was incomplete, but I was able to assemble the pieces. I wrote down what I heard and said goodbye. I never asked the boy his name, and it never even occurred to me to do so. I just wanted to reassure him that he was heard, and I did just that. The picture of the little brown-haired boy and his mother, a young, blonde-haired, blue-eyed woman, slowly faded from my view.

Three days passed before I made the effort to try again. I sat down on the floor, legs crossed, and closed my eyes. Not long afterward, I saw Polaroid pictures fly from left to right. I didn't complain or ask anyone to slow down, and I didn't succumb to frustration either. I began to notice a pattern in these photos; they all were children. Colored photos of small babies popped into my purview, but without a narrative to share. Some children struggled to speak and give their message. They sounded as if they were reaching for a clean breath. I could not understand why they were appearing, but I allowed them to pierce through the veil.

Initially, I was confused and curious about these encounters; I wanted to share them and find some sort of clarity or understanding about what was happening. Was meditation the gateway to these experiences? Although I did not explore the world of psychics, I knew about mediumship, but I did not know how that worked. I wanted a different perspective about what was occurring. My relationship with my parents was completely strained. At this point in my life, I could not lean on my stepmother or share my life with her. Since she met me at the age of six, she'd kept me at a safe distance. My biological mother was not in my life, and my father lacked the necessary skills to communicate on all levels, especially emotionally.

As mentioned earlier, I have three sisters: Nicole, the eldest, Beatrice, my stepsister who became a sanctified Pentecostal Christian, and Casey, the youngest. While I shared my experiences with my sister Nicole, I wanted a religious explanation, as if that was somehow closer to the truth. I sought this explanation from Beatrice. While dialing her phone number, I felt a knot in my stomach slowly tightening; for a split second I thought about hanging up the phone. Did I really want to share these visions, these voices, and the secrets of my life with her? While the phone rang, I dramatized what I was going to say. How would I explain this to her, a devoted Christian, that my heart was pulling me to seek elsewhere, gravitating toward a new road?

Beatrice answered the phone and we spoke. I casually asked her about her day to set a calm precedent for the conversation. During a dull silence, I took the opportunity to bring up the dead children. I explained to my sister that I had been practicing meditation during which I had visions of deceased children. I further explained to her that I could hear them speak to me. These words simply rolled off my tongue, and I could not contain them. There was a long pause on the other end. I waited nervously for her reply. I loved my sister, but I greatly feared her response. Out of the four of us, Beatrice was the only saved Christian. I assumed, just by that alone, that she possessed some mystical connection that endowed her with special gifts and knowledge that I would never be privy to on account of my being unsaved.

Swiftly, my sister told me that she did not know who I was praying to, or what sort of meditation I was doing, but all she knew was that she prayed to God. That knot in my stomach tightened, and I felt anger rise in my chest. Was she really implying that I was not praying to God, *her* God? There was such an overt condemnation present in her voice and in her words, I felt she had already crucified me. I was speechless. I could only think to say that I wanted to share my experiences with her to get her opinion, and then hung up the phone. That was the first and last time I have ever shared my experiences with her. Lesson learned.

I did not bother to meditate every day. I was still unclear about its purpose, and I did not have a clear vision of my intentions. This was a big mistake, and I did not realize the possible consequences of opening up to the spirit world without protection. On a day like any other, I learned a valuable and frightening lesson that would temporarily cost me peace of mind.

One particular day at the beginning of this journey, I returned home early from school in the afternoon and decided to meditate, utilizing the same process. I sat down with legs crossed and closed my eyes. The dark veil slowly parted from my view. A steady stream of pictures flew in from right to left across my sight, but nothing "exceptional" popped out toward my focus. A surge of exhaustion seized my body, and I decided to take a short nap, which for me was a rare occurrence based on the simple fact that I did not like to take naps because they made me feel groggy afterward.

I lay my head on a pillow on my little green-and-white-striped sofa and closed my eyes soon afterward. I fell into a comfortable, deep, coma-like sleep. Within fifteen minutes I felt a tug on my velvet, rose-printed blanket, that was spread across my body. It took a minute or two to realize what was happening. I felt multiple wild tugs on the corners of the blanket; I was forcefully being pulled down off the couch. In desperation, I tried to jab my shoulders forward, but the harder I tried, the harder I was being pulled. I fell onto the floor next to my couch and attempted to kick my legs, but to no avail. My eyes felt as if they were taped shut, and I struggled to open them. I felt myself being kicked on my legs and shoulders, but I was paralyzed and helpless. I directed my focus toward my mouth and tried to scream, but my cheeks were anesthetized and my tongue was officially disarmed.

I prayed, asking God for the mobility of my mouth, my hands, and my legs. The mighty hand of God did not reach down to lift me up from the floor; instead, I felt an overwhelming surge of weightlessness envelop me. I continued to feel the density of my body, but I knew I was simultaneously floating above it. While the eyes of my body remained sealed, my soul encompassed an aerial perspective of the situation at hand. The body below was intentionally being held down, but I did not possess the ability to discern who or what it was. In a swift moment, I shifted my gaze toward the living-room window. Seconds later, a shadowy outline of a small figure toddled to my window and ran to kick my face. Suddenly, my head popped backward onto the floor. The fear instantly dissipated and my chest began to swell in anger. Shortly thereafter, golden rays of light stabbed through the living-room floor and erupted over my paralytic body, molding into the shape of a pyramid. Immediately my head fell back and light appeared to rise from the center of the Earth and encased my body in the shape of a pyramid. I was convinced I was hallucinating.

Still floating in stasis above my body, I saw a three-dimensional pyramid of light hugging my small frame from head to toe. I retreated into this stranded body as these entities fought to keep me paralyzed. I lay there, engulfed in a pyramid, when caroling rays of golden light darted out of each face of the pyramid. The blanket fell limp onto my body and my captors disappeared. My arms flailed wildly about my body and my mouth fell open, exhausted from my unsuccessful attempts to scream. My legs were shaky, but I managed to pull myself off the floor and back onto the couch. I jumped up off the floor frightened, surprised, and relieved. I looked about me only to find no captors. Clearly I had opened a door of which I was completely ignorant. The fear arrested my spirit, and that experience stifled and incapacitated my spiritual progress, but only temporarily.

The depth of my guilt fluctuated after this frightening incident. Perhaps my sister was correct. Maybe I was serving a different master and had abandoned God in his entirety. I didn't meditate for some time after that incident. I slipped into my old mode of fear-based thinking. I, again, relied on Christ as my lord and savior and supreme protector against all things evil. My Christianity had once again become my safety net.

Months passed and I had fallen back into my old routine of going to the gym, to school, and then home to read, write, grade, and sleep. My sister Nicole called me one day to speak to me about her ongoing divorce. She lived in Arizona then and was fighting a tough battle with her husband. She invited me to visit her in the next few months to spend some time together with her, her children, and my mother, whom I had not seen in twenty years. I definitely took her up on her offer. I loved to travel and explore, and I truly hated living in Texas and willingly utilized any excuse I could to leave that state.

After finishing summer excavations in Belize, I escaped to Arizona. Upon arrival I found Nicole to be in a scary situation. Her divorce was incredibly difficult, and she felt completely abandoned by everyone she loved. We spent many days traveling through Flagstaff and Sedona rehashing our youth. To me, it felt like a period of growth and healing between sisters.

While visiting Nicole, I felt the urge to try meditating again. I felt safe in her apartment, and I figured if anything did happen, she would be a witness, and of course, she could rescue me. For privacy, I walked to the bathroom, closed the door, and sat down on the tile floor. I have to admit that I was incredibly nervous to try again. I still truly believed I had been attacked by demons.

Sitting on the bathroom floor, I closed my eyes. Patiently, I waited for something to happen. Two or three minutes into my meditation, I felt electrical currents surge throughout my body, beginning at my feet and then pulsing up my legs and torso and through the crown of my head. My whole body began to vibrate and rock sharply back and forth. The lids of my eyes fluttered wildly like butterfly wings as pulses of energy billowed up my spine. My body began to pulsate faster, and the light in the room expanded across my vision. I took in a series of deep breaths and exhaled to release the intense energy coursing through my being. I looked about me with eyes closed to find the room washed with golden light. And then the second wave hit. Pulses of energy climbed the jagged edges of my vertebrae, curved around my spine, and raced out of the crown of my head. I squinted because the light was too bright. I instantly opened my eyes only to find that the light in the room was not bright at all.

Feeling safe, I meditated almost every day I visited with my sister, and each time my experience was the same. As an amateur, I partially believed that this was what enlightenment was supposed to look like. I obviously had no prior knowledge of what I have now come to understand as the enlightenment process. I returned to Texas a few weeks later. I felt completely refreshed and alive. A fire had been lit in my mind, and it was ready to burst into flames.

Every semester I counted down the days until I finished my PhD. Although my trip to Arizona provided a long-awaited break, it also reminded me of the fact that I had not been living my life. In school I felt on edge, sad, and disappointed. I was caught in a web of competition between women in my cohort; this was definitely not what I had envisioned my experience to be like. I constantly sought something outside myself to help me, to show me what I was living for, to be my guiding light. I never found it in any of the books I read, and I couldn't successfully find it in the people I dated or worked with. I just wanted to give up and surrender, and I forgot why I even went to graduate school in the first place. Most days I was on autopilot. I woke up, went to the gym, drove to school, attended my classes, worked until 1 a.m., and then went to bed.

Believe it or not, I did not meditate when I returned from Arizona. There was residual Christian guilt and palpable fear that still arose after my last frightening experience. I was also alone. There was no one to protect me if I was to be attacked again. The voices came to me intermittently at night, and I continued to ignore them. Every time I heard my name called in the darkest hours of the night, I prayed and asked it to please go away.

Months passed and the regularity of my life bored me. I succumbed to the blues brought on by school and work. One hot summer day in Texas, which is a normal day, I took my usual hurried walk onto campus to get to my class, when I noticed a man with shiny sable skin. Undoubtedly, he walked toward me with a purpose. This man was wearing a backward conference badge, so I couldn't see his name or which conference he was attending. He had a sweet smile on his face and walked toward me self-assured. He planted his feet in front of me and said, "Hello." My old self was a bit uncomfortable meeting new people at times. I feared judgment, and my perception of my own self-worth was worsening the more time I spent in graduate school. However, in this particular instance, I was alert and secure. Feeling no pressure to perform, I simply said, "Hello," in return. He asked me how I was doing and I said I was okay. That was my truth at the time. I had been okay, although I felt my neck was barely above water. He stated he had been at the college campus only for that day and wanted to explain what he noticed. I was completely interested in his opinion, and I wondered if it mirrored mine at all. He proceeded to report that he saw the level of vanity, superficiality, and competition at this university and explained how he knew it was challenging and burdensome. I nodded furiously in agreement. My colleagues, I felt, or as I had perceived them then, were extremely combative, cutthroat, competitive, and vain. I did not know how to thrive in that sort of environment, and I allowed it to eat away at my being day by day. This kind man further relayed to me, "God wants you to know that you can do anything, anything you want; did you know that? Anything you want." This statement startled me. I acknowledged that I understood because, truthfully, I *did* understand.

Despite the message I received, my lifestyle didn't change. I lacked a clear vision regarding the direction of my life, but I knew that the road I had been traveling did not allow for the cultivation of my dreams. Between research and teaching, I briefly focused my attention inward in an attempt to discern the vectors of my truest desires. I carefully explored the corridors of this alternate reality that could be my life, one where I lived joyfully and courageously through the heart. I gave myself permission to psychologically orbit this surrogate identity and found it wholly appealing. Although I desperately wanted to embody this utopian existence, I decided to complete the PhD program. However, I was not yet willing to surrender my dreams, and I boldly made the decision that being an archaeologist would not be the route of my soul.

Knowing that this was not my path made waking up in the morning and going to school even harder. Unbeknown to me, my guardian angels were in great agreement with my decision and knew something I had not. In an arduous attempt to garner my attention, they delivered messages to me via my watch, phone, and alarm clock. It took about one and a half weeks until I noticed the repetitive number appearing on all of my devices. In the morning my clock read

9:11. At night, my watch read "9:11." While driving, the license plates of unruly commuter vehicles read 911. I finally stated aloud in my bedroom to no one in particular, "I don't know what this means!" Frustrated, I also yelled, "I don't know *anyone* who died on 9/11."

This, however, did not deter the incoming messages, of course. At that time, I was not akin to messages of spirit, but my intuition knew that something was up. I saw this message so often that I finally confided in Nicole. Neither of us really knew what to do, so our natural reaction was to just ignore it, since neither of us knew anyone even related to a person who experienced the tragedy of 9/11. These digits became a recurring theme in my life. My watch conveniently always read 9:11. Unknown to me, this was an overt message from above. A few years later I would come to know the meaning of this message from the angels encouraging me to pursue my life purpose and soul mission as a light worker.

My mission during that phase in my life consisted of surviving my PhD program with my sanity intact. I was living in a perpetual state of fear. Fear takes many forms, including sadness, worry, complaint, denial, anxiety, and anger, and I battled them all every day, all day. My social life also suffered during these years. I had only one person in my life whom I could truly call my friend and confidant. I casually dated, but I was not ready to establish a committed relationship with anyone.

After I finished taking all of my coursework in the program and my fieldwork in Belize, I spent more time at home and at the gym. I came to the conclusion that the university setting was a toxic environment, and I refused to go unless required. Within weeks I mentally felt better. I no longer felt exhausted from having to protect myself from others. I no longer operated within a defensive mode. I began to try to enjoy my life by eating out with my friend, going to the movies, and getting a personal trainer at the gym. Although I still had to complete my dissertation, I felt relieved due to the changes I'd made.

Unexpectedly during the last year of my coursework, I began dating again and met a kind, generous, and compassionate man. He was attending the same university, which was convenient. We studied together in the evening, and he took me out to explore nature sites during the weekends. Within a few weeks, we were practically living together. In my heart, he was familiar, and I was genuinely happy. After five months of dating, however, he told me that he was moving back home to California upon graduation. He had lived in Texas for several years and knew this was not the place he wanted to spend the rest of his life.

I was deeply hurt and angry. Why did he wait to tell me? My response was swift. I thanked him for the good times and offered him good luck. He was shocked. That was definitely not what he had hoped for. He expressed his desire to maintain a long-distance relationship. Instantly I said no. I had experienced these types of relationships before and believed they did not work. It took me a few weeks to muster up the strength to speak my truth. I wanted a relationship but adamantly refused to have a long-distance one. I wondered how this could work. I had already taken a summer teaching position at the university, which I needed, but he was leaving in May. After a few weeks of thinking, I finally made him a proposition, but I worried about his response. I sat him down and told him that if we truly wanted a committed relationship, I would have to move there. After serious discussion, we decided that I would move to California after having finished my summer teaching job. At that time, I was nervous and excited. I drove with my boyfriend to California, spent time with his family, and flew back to Texas to finish my job. Little did I know that once I moved, my life as I knew it would change considerably.

It took a lot of bribing to convince my best friend, Ava, to drive with me from Texas to California. It was going to be a long drive ahead of us, but I was moving forward in the direction of my destiny.

I officially settled into Scotts Valley, California, a few months later. I spent my days writing my dissertation and explored the Santa Cruz beaches during the weekend. At the beginning, there were initial growing pains, as there are in any new relationship. One particular evening, we had a terrible argument, and I was beginning to question whether or not I had made a mistake after all. While my boyfriend was at work, I sat at home very upset and worried that I had abandoned everything and everyone I knew for someone who might not want to accept me. During the afternoon, I sat amid a pile of textbooks and was overcome with fear and anxiety. I was afraid of being humiliated and embarrassed if I had to return home.

I sat on the floor crying uncontrollably, asking God why this was happening. After about ten minutes, the tears stopped; I wiped my face and remained seated on the floor. I closed my eyes and asked quietly, "Why am I here? Was this a mistake?" I was breathing heavily, not thinking, not expecting to hear an answer. Within a few minutes I felt my head jerk backward and the room turned a light shade of blue. I heard a voice in the room that sounded as if it was broadcasting through an old CB radio from a long-haul driving truck. Through the static I heard the voice speak, "Denana." Without fear or shock, and maybe with some arrogance, I replied, "Nope. That's not my name."

I felt a presence sitting right behind me and heard what I could distinguish as a male voice. Through the static it stated, "It's so simple." Offended, I retorted, "Simple? What's so simple?" The voice responded, "No, it's *not* so simple, but this is your destiny." Upon hearing those words, I froze, realizing that I had clearly been hearing voices and had been conversing with them. My eyelids quickly flipped open and I stood up and walked out the room confused. I wasn't sure if I even believed in destiny, and I knew that those were definitely not my words. Who was speaking to me and why were they there? And why was the room painted sky blue? I was not entirely convinced that Scotts Valley, California, was my destiny.

The next morning, I sat in the same spot with my eyes closed, hoping to determine whether or not I had actually heard a voice or if it was my imagination. At least ten minutes had passed when I heard a dull voice struggling to speak. I said, "Hello," and asked for clarification about what was said the previous day. There was a short pause and then a voice broke through. "I will tell you, but first, you have to do something for me." I was taken aback by the request. Intuitively, I knew something was wrong. The previous day's message had carried a certain type of energy, and this message felt uncomfortable. Hesitantly, I replied, "Okay. First, who is this?" A slew of names were thrown in my direction, none of them familiar. The last name frightened me: "Beelzebub."

My heart pounded heavily in my chest, I placed my hand on it in an attempt to slow it down. Upon hearing that name, I began to pray. I felt an overwhelming sense of fear and familiar guilt in my heart at that moment. Maybe my sister was right; maybe I *had* been consorting with the Devil. I knew I would not attempt to do this again. The reality of what I had been playing with scared me, and I believed that my actions were wrong, and most likely frowned upon by God. I sat on the floor as a true sinner.

As I lay in bed, I worried about my actions that day. Had I invited the Devil into my life? That night I fell asleep and had a dream that confirmed my fears. I dreamed that I was with a team on another archaeological excavation. For some reason, I had split up from the group and found myself lost in the forest. I turned to my left and then my right and saw only a cluster of forest trees and scattered branches. I slowly turned around to find a clear pathway but instead saw a big, black lion staring at me in the distance. I was frightened. Instinctively, I knew the lion was coming for me, and I took off running as fast as I could. The trees became a massive blur of green and brown hues as I struggled to get away. My right foot twisted beneath me and I tripped and fell over a large tree root. Scurrying on the ground I turned around to find the lion only a few feet away from me. I crawled slowly like a crab away from him as his eyes pierced mine. As I crawled, my right wrist twisted and my hand slipped on a thick pile of dead leaves. The lion slowly walked toward me until his mane was deliberately a few inches from tickling my face. His eyes were shining a dirty yellow color. The faint sound of a broken twig cracked in the distance before he could wound me. Irritated, the lion turned its head to look at what caused the noise. That was my moment. I took off running deeper into the forest. I knew that whatever, or whoever, had distracted the lion so that I could escape.

At this stage in the process, I had been incredibly naive, and even lazy. I never took the time to research proper methods of meditation and communication with spirit. I learned the hard way. This dream confirmed my fear of working with the "spirit world." I believed I had transgressed God, and I was being punished for it.

The next few months were filled with intense research and writing. Regardless of how I felt, I persevered and began to crank out chapters and even apply to university teaching positions. My mind logically told me that this was the way to secure my financial future, and that sometimes life meant doing what you do not like to live. As I progressed through my writing, that thought gradually solidified in my mind and became my reality.

Throughout this process, my heart and head were in an unremitting rivalry. My heart cried for a miracle, and my mind convinced me to stick to my commitment and persevere. I diligently organized my time and dedicated myself to completing several chapters. Although my boyfriend and I had loved living near Santa Cruz, spending our weekend at the beaches and exploring the coastline, we unexpectedly moved to San Francisco to sublease a house from his best friend.

CHAPTER 4

Communication

The house we moved into was a yellow, two-story Victorian built in 1905, which remained structurally sound after the devastating 1906 Earthquake. Our new home was located near many tourist shops and the lush greenery that is Golden Gate Park. Although we moved to San Francisco, Noah still worked in the heart of Silicon Valley. I knew absolutely nothing about the city except that driving around it was truly a nightmare.

Noah used multiple forms of public transportation to and from work, spending a majority of his day on the road. Therefore, I spent many days alone writing and exploring the gardens and lakes of neighboring parks. At this point, I had been in graduate school for six years, and I was determined to finish as soon as possible. I honestly could not bear spending another minute reading about the ancient Maya; boredom engulfed every inch of my being. Communication with my friends and family was a rare occurrence, so when I felt the need to articulate my frustration, I spoke to God directly. Day in and day out, I exhausted myself complaining about how much I hated writing my dissertation, how I disliked the college program, and even lamenting how I had made such a big mistake wasting my time and energy on something I no longer believed would help anyone in reality. As I typed my chapters, I cried and grumbled about the path I had chosen. My heart was dissatisfied with the choices I'd made, and knew better my deepest desires, which did not include spending the rest of my life as an academic professor. My ego's desire to succeed as a top-notch professor was slowly but surely crumbling.

During the lonely hours in this new house, a quiet but persistent voice inside me encouraged me to *try, try, try* again. Meditate. My previous experiences meditating were both good and bad. I assumed that dark spirits were trying to communicate with me again, and I was extremely hesitant. I knew I was still not saved or sanctified by any church to commune with otherworldly light beings. But I still felt a determined inner nudge. There were many mornings I sat in our dining room, which had then become my huge dissertation-writing room, debating about meditation. This inner voice was relentless, and no matter how hard I tried to silence it, it never left me. I enjoyed living in that house, but I knew I was not alone. Occasionally during the day and in the middle of the night, I heard heavy footsteps down the hall, causing the hardwood floors to creak. Other times, I heard the tail-end whisper of my name. Although I wanted to practice meditating, I was afraid.

About one month after we moved to San Francisco, I opted to reach for the courage to try meditating again. I supposed spirits were trying to communicate with me, but I did not know why. After all, I had been hearing them all my life but lacked the understanding and practical know-how to respond. Intuitively, I knew that meditating would facilitate spiritual dialogue. I declared to whoever or whatever was present that I would begin with only five minutes a day, and dependent upon that, I would increase it to ten minutes a day the following week. Anxiously, I sat down in front of the bay window in the dining room and prayed for protection. After taking a deep breath, I closed my eyes for a whole five minutes. I saw nothing and felt a sense of relief. That evening before I went to bed, I prayed for more protection as I slept.

In the early morning hours I helped Noah leave the house on time and went for a run in the park. Upon returning, I sat down and completed my newly devised five-minute meditation. Sitting with my legs folded, I prayed for protection and closed my eyes for five minutes. I felt victorious every time I finished. I saw nothing but felt triumphant. That week, I managed to meditate every day successfully for five minutes. The following week, I decided to increase my meditation to ten minutes a day, and this time I included music.

Although I successfully conquered the five-minute meditation, I did not quite like the idea of being alone in that house in darkness with my eyes closed for ten minutes. As a solution, I imagined being on horseback riding in the colorful Arizona desert, which I enjoyed but had never done in real life. Upon completing the meditation, I felt happy and, more importantly, safe. About two days into my ten-minute meditation practice, a man unexpectedly appeared in the desert. He was a sleek, long-haired Native American man who saddled up our horses and rode alongside me. At first, I chose not to question who he was or even why he was there. I simply enjoyed his company and said goodbye when I was ready to leave. During my third meditation, we rode to a specific destination. He tied up our horses and led me to a little campfire near the edge of a red rock cliff. I sat down on a small blanket by the fire and gazed out into the desert sky. My mind drifted as I admired the purple and burnt-red hues crystallized in the large rock formations. Interrupting my thoughts, this man asked me to focus and stare into the fire pit. Without hesitation, I looked down into the flames, but without fail, my mind succumbed to distracting thoughts about school and writing. This man appeared daily in my meditations, and each time, I attempted to focus on the flames in the fire pit; some days I was successful, and others, not so much. I met this man for an additional two weeks to practice and strengthen my focus. Little had I known that this practice, and my courage to explore new spiritual territory, would open a door to reclaiming my divine birthright.

I have to say that I was incredibly proud of myself. I meditated successfully for four weeks total without an incident. Although I knew spirits were attached to this house, because I could feel them, I was courageous enough to close my eyes and meditate for an entire ten to fifteen minutes each day. Nothing and no one had touched me, held me down, kicked me, or attempted to scare me. While I was still uncertain about my end goal, there was a persistent voice encouraging me to continue trying. And I did.

I was unaware that through my meditative practice, I was opening the gateway to my spiritual abilities and a door to spirit communication. I was by all means an amateur. One significant evening, months after meditating, Noah and I lay down for bed. He was exhausted from traveling to Mountain View, and I was spent from writing and researching all day. That night I closed my eyes to fall asleep and, unbeknown to me, after that night my life would never be the same as I understood it. The universe finds every way possible to communicate with us. For some, spiritual communication manifests in the form of colors, animals, coins, or repetitive songs. One of the quintessential methods of spirit communication involves penetrating our dream state, and the universe, God, and my guide approached me during my REM cycle. That evening I dreamed Noah and I were walking down the hallway in our new house toward our dining room. As we walked in the room, Noah grabbed his heart and fell onto the hardwood floor. I ran toward him and began screaming uncontrollably for help. I believed he was having a heart attack. Noah closed his eyes, asked me to stop screaming, took a deep breath, and relayed to me he was okay. I took a short step back from his body and realized that he was not having a heart attack after all. I was puzzled; what was happening to him?

I stood there staring at Noah lying on the ground, trying to comprehend what had just transpired. In response to my confusion, he said, "This is how I tell you I love you, this is how I tell you I love you. Find something to write with." I ran over to the mirror hanging above the wooden mantel, breathed on it, and wrote the symbols he dictated to me. About two symbols in, Noah demanded that I find an actual pen to write with, emphasizing that I would forget upon waking. Quickly, I darted around the room to locate a pen but grabbed my sage bundle instead. I burned it and began to draw all the symbols on the mirror. To my memory, I drew at least twenty symbols. He asked if I would remember, and I said, "Yes."

I woke up the next morning at 6:00, made coffee, and helped Noah leave the house on time. I carried on as usual and, of course, had completely forgotten the entire dream. After a run in the park, I returned home and turned on the radio to listen to a show about energy centers in the body. During the show, I heard the hosts discuss symbology in association with balancing the chakras, and I instantly remembered my dream. Excited, I picked up the phone, called my best friend, Ava, and recounted my dream to her. Unfortunately, I could remember only two of the symbols I drew on the mirror.

These are the following symbols shown to me in my dream (see figures 1 and 2).

Ava and I researched the meaning behind the circumpunct and the pyramid, only to find that these two symbols had assorted cultural meanings. What exactly was this message? And who was it who told me this is how they love me? Feeling overwhelmed by the level of information, we stopped our search. Although I was unbelievably excited by my dream and the symbols, I still had a dissertation to complete. I hung up the phone, looked at the stack of books on my table, and sighed. How much longer did I have to subject myself to this? I decided not to open another research book. These symbols ignited the fire of inquisition within my being, and I was determined to discover their meaning.

Fig. 1 Circumpunct as represented in my dreams.

Fig. 2 Pyramid as represented in my dreams.

I walked away from the long, wooden dining table, sat on the white love seat, and flipped through my Kindle. For the past six years my bookshelves were stacked with anthropology and archaeology texts, and I was dying to read something nonacademic. I had recently purchased a catalog of metaphysical books I planned to devour after my graduation. I flipped to the book *Pyramids of Light: Awakening to Multi-dimensional Realities*, by Meg Blackburn Losey,[1] and gave myself permission to indulge in something unrelated to the Maya before I returned to my dissertation research. The first few pages of this book were dense, and I was certain I lacked the mental capacity to understand the text. I persevered, as I always do, and carefully read the words aloud. Truthfully, I felt the book was above my mental pay grade. For a single minute, I doubted my ability to grasp what was being presented, and became frustrated. Before closing the book, I encouraged myself to skim through the pages before totally giving up.

I was positively unprepared for the information presented in the following pages. Within these pages lie the two symbols from my dream. I read the author's definitions for understanding. According to Losey, the circumpunct can be explained as follows:

"the sphere represents a never-ending connection with its exterior enclosing infinite possibilities. It also represents our consciousness and us as beings."[2]

The dot in the center

"acts as a guidance point and balances the sphere."[3]

Losey states,

"*without some sort of guidance in the center of the circle, the interior is energetically chaotic with all of the possibilities bouncing off the circular walls with no anchoring energy or direction. When inserted into the center of the sphere, the dot is representative of the balance we find in ourselves when we allow spirit, or light, to guide us.*"[4]

The pyramid, on the other hand, is a common cross-cultural symbol with assorted meanings and interpretations. Losey writes that the pyramid is the

"*basic form of the universal construct. The upright four-sided pyramid is representative of our consciousness. It is the true trinity of being.*"[5]

I took this message to mean that I, like the sphere, am an eternal being containing, within myself, unlimited potential. However, I must trust spirit to be my center and guiding light. The pyramid symbolized my eternal makeup that embodies the power, wisdom, and light of the Father, Son, and Holy Spirit. I was greatly shocked and humbled by this revelation. During my life journey, thus far, I did not believe in coincidences. I believed, as pedestrian as this may sound, that everything occurred for a reason and at the right time. Honestly, I still did not know who was providing me with this information, but I knew it was a holy entity trying to communicate or provide a message, and my heart was inundated with gratitude and appreciation. While my ego was trying to impregnate me with doubt and skepticism, the joy of my heart overpowered any self-doubt or self-attack. After this experience, my heart and mind became insatiable. I wanted to spend every second of the day researching anything and everything; I truly did not know where to begin. I reminded myself that I still had to complete my dissertation and balance my life. I outlined every minute of the day in order to guarantee that I had time to write, meditate, research, and cook and clean. In an attempt to satiate my metaphysical appetite, I listened to a variety of podcasts about God, creation, the law of attraction, near-death experiences, crystals, and almost anything you could ever imagine. My soul took a hearty leap of faith that day.

During the first few weeks after seeing these symbols, I bought a sizable collection of metaphysical books. I was overcome with interest in all things spiritual. It felt as if someone had kindled a light in my heart and my mind, and

I was soulfully energized. My dissertation was completed between my studies and comparisons of various spiritual texts.

At the beginning stages of my research, I felt overwhelmed by the nature and amount of available metaphysical content. I read a wide array of books on the chakras, or energy centers in the body, and a compendium of literature about the afterlife. This information forced me to reevaluate my existing beliefs and question my habitual way of thinking. While I could accept and believe in the possibility of an afterlife, and even that our bodies housed a spirit with an electrical energy system, I maintained a healthy dose of skepticism regarding some of the hallmarks of the New Age movement; namely, crystals. I've seen New Age devotees adorn their bodies with different crystals, which matched their free-spirited tie-dye dresses and alternative hippie gear. Admittedly, I was suspicious and doubtful about the function and power of crystals. I listened to podcasts where the hosts swore by the healing energy of crystals. Did stones or crystals carry and transmit energy? After all, these are inanimate objects. I found it difficult to expand my mind to believe these theories. Given the depth of my metaphysical research, I was becoming well aware of the emphasis placed on crystals as Earthen forms that contain healing energy. I cannot say why this in particular bothered me so much. Were men worshiping these false idols? I was concerned that material possessions, such as crystals, were obfuscating the search for the truth of my identity. I prayed and asked for confirmation or proof that this was even a possibility.

Again, it was in the world of dreams where my questions were answered. That evening, I dreamed I was on a work field trip with a group of people walking in a single-file line. However, I was driven to deviate from the line and follow a woman with short red hair and gray pants. She was carrying something in her pocket that I knew belonged to me. Finally, after much following, I was able to catch up with the woman and demanded that she give me what was already mine. I desperately had to have it. The redheaded woman pulled a large chunk of rose quartz out of her right pocket; I snatched it from her hands and ran.

Although the universe provided me with confirmation about the power and legitimacy of crystal work, I still functioned in the mindset of disbelief. Did I really need rose quartz and should I be wearing it around my neck? That morning I looked online for stones of my liking to purchase. I loved the colors purple and blue. I thought, why not, and purchased several pendants. Additionally, I purchased a clear quartz and rose quartz pendant along with a large lapis lazuli necklace. My ego obviously wanted what it wanted and completely ignored the guidance of my dream.

Three days later, I received all pendants and my necklace in the mail. The stones and crystals were beautiful, and I could not wait to wear them. That morning, I had a number of errands to run around the neighborhood, and I was eager to show off my new gems. I placed lapis lazuli around my neck and walked right out the door down the street to the post office. The stone looked beautiful against my white shirt, and I was proud to wear it. I almost made it down to the post office doors when the clasp of my necklace broke. To my surprise, I caught the necklace and stone before it fell to the sidewalk. Immediately, I was stunned and angry. I had just purchased this necklace; why did it break? Unknowingly, this was a sign from above.

When I returned home, I found an old sterling-silver chain and decided to try a different stone. My eyes scanned the pendants I had just received in the mail, and I picked up the amethyst and placed it on the chain. Satisfied with my selection, I grabbed my purse and left the house to complete my errands. On my way home from the market I felt something slip down my shirt. My grocery bag slipped out of my hand and I dropped my purse onto the sidewalk. I looked below at the pavement, and to my amazement I saw the silver chain and amethyst pendant below me. Angrily, I shoved the amethyst and chain in my jeans pocket and walked home. When I arrived home, I found a new silver chain and attached the rose quartz pendant. Needless to say, the chain did not break. The following week I listened to a podcast where a leading female psychic discussed how budding intuitives are always guided to wear rose quartz when opening to spirit at the beginning of their journey to open their heart. I looked around the kitchen room and said, "Thank you. Lesson learned."

In my spare time, I continued my quest for knowledge. One very instrumental book in my development was *The Psychic Pathway*, by Sonia Choquette.[6] As I read this book, I became intrigued about the proposed idea that everyone is psychic. She explained that to be psychic was to be "of the soul."[7] And one thing I knew for sure was that we all were souls. Before committing to this book, I wanted to find psychics or, at the very least, mystics in the Bible to reassure me that this work was legit and holy consecrated. According to my understanding, psychics commune with the divine to provide messages, celestial assistance, and healing to the people of the Earth. They work directly with the source that is God. Psychic work involves the utilization of phenomena unexplained by natural laws, including clairvoyance, clairaudience, and even clairsentience. Clairvoyance means clear seeing, whereby an individual has visions that may reveal future events in order to warn people or provide supportive messages to those in need. In ancient society, clairvoyants were simply called seers. Clairaudience is defined as clear hearing; an individual with this gift can hear spirits with their external ears or hear internally through telepathic communication. Clairsentience simply means clear feeling, or clear sensing, whereby a person can sense energy or feel another person's emotions and energy; they have the true gift of sensing and discerning various forms of energy. Psychics rely on these gifts, as well as tools of divination, to assist the progress of the soul. I expected to identify psychics in the Bible who embodied one or more of these gifts, to reassure me that psychic work is condoned and supported by God.

In my quest for understanding, I learned that some seers, those who have the gift of clairvoyance, or sight, and see visions given by God, were prophets as reflected in the Old Testament. Others are clearly identified only as seers, a person whose mode of communion with God was through sight. Seers are identified in the Bible by the Hebrew words *Ro'eh* and *Chozeh*, which can be found in the Book of Samuel.[8] One of the main "duties" of the prophet/seer, in the Old Testament, was to reveal God's messages to the people. Their gifts enabled them to predict the future, either by vision or by hearing God speak, relating to God's punishment/wrath due to the sins of the people. Additionally, these messages were conveyed as warnings for the people to obey the word of God. Other prophetic messages provided insight into God's plan for the people. Some of these messages encouraged the righteous people of God.[9]

One of the most renowned prophets in the Old Testament was Jeremiah. To provide some context, Jeremiah was designated a prophet and messenger of God. His messages were provided through his gift of sight, which were revealed through visual impressions. At the beginning of the book of Jeremiah, God asks Jeremiah twice what he sees.[10] In response, Jeremiah describes two symbolic visions representing messages of God that he was commanded to bring to the people of Judah. It can also be assumed that this prophet possessed the gift of clairaudience, meaning that he heard with his external ears the messages of God as God spoke to him throughout this book.

Another gifted seer in the Old Testament was named Iddo. Iddo is *specifically* identified as a seer, who lived in the land of Judah and had prophetic visions.[11] Gad was an important seer for King David of Israel, as noted in 1 Chronicles and 1 and 2 Samuel.[12] Gad not only possessed the gift of clairvoyance, but likely had clairaudience, the ability to hear spirits, as it is stated in 1 Samuel, "*When David arose in the morning, the word of the lord God came to the prophet Gad, David's seer.*"[13]

A female seer by the name of Huldah, a prophetess in Jerusalem, is also mentioned briefly in 2 Kings.[14] As presented in the Bible, God communicated through Huldah, and many officials sought her out for the messages of God. In one particular instance, King Josiah sent his priest, scribe, and official to Huldah for confirmation of the word of God and to determine the possible impending destruction if they chose to ignore it. In the Hebrew Bible, the role of Huldah is magnified, since she was heavily relied upon by kings to inquire about the fate of their nation.[15] The prophet Samuel was bestowed the gift of hearing spirits, since it is stated that he heard voices call his name only to learn that it was the voice of God.[16] In 1 Chronicles, Samuel is also identified as a seer.[17]

One important thing to reiterate is the role that these psychics or prophets played, as reflected in 2 Kings: "*Yet the Lord warned Israel and Judah through all his prophets and every seer, saying, turn from your evil ways and keep my commandments, my statues according to all the laws which I commanded your father, and which I sent to you through my servants, the prophets.*"[18]

Lastly, the prophet Isaiah was a messenger of God who judged and warned those who had turned their backs on God about God's wrath. He prophesized during the reigns of Uzziah, Jotham, Ahaz, and Hezekiah, the kings of Judah. Isaiah also had the gift of clairvoyance and acted as a seer—he was shown visions from God to relay to the people.[19] He directly communicated and heard the voice of God as he delivered his messages forth.

The terms "seer" and "prophet" are later conflated in the Old Testament: "*Before time in Israel, when a man went to inquire of God, thus he spake, Come and let us go to the seer; for he that is now called a prophet was before time called a seer.*"[20] In the New Testament, the term "seer" is absent. However, prophets in the New Testament continued to have visions of Heaven, including Stephen, John, and Paul, as a form of divine communion.

Knowing that so many prophets or seers legitimately performed psychic work, were accepted in their society, and were later revered eased some of my fears and initial skepticism. It was particularly Samuel's experience of hearing God repeatedly call his name that provided me comfort as I transitioned into this work. Intuitively I knew that the age of prophets or psychics was alive and well. At no point had I read that the role of the prophet or seer died once the Bible was canonized. Nor were there any official decrees announcing the extinction of God's desire to communicate with and through us as his holy children on Earth.

Feeling more comfortable, I progressed through Choquette's book. Midway through I found that a few psychic tools, such as the Tarot and pendulums, were introduced as divination tools, and I was particularly hesitant to use them. I had been taught during my childhood that such tools were tools of the Devil, and I most certainly did not embrace them immediately. Sonia discusses how these tools actually assist in the expansion of our awareness and allow us to tap into the collective consciousness or "*invisible field that surrounds the planet, in which all gathered knowledge is available.*"[21] She further explains that our "*soul is ancient and recognizes these tools as familiar symbols. These symbols resonate with your deepest soul awareness, bypassing the logical mind and its limitations.*"[22]

I prayed constantly for clarity and guidance about utilizing such divination paraphernalia. I feared repercussions from dabbling into what I believed comprised the dark arts, or witchcraft. My perception at that time had been shaped by stereotypical depictions of fortune tellers and biblical scriptures condemning witches and sorcerers. During prayer, I expressed to God that I had no intention, or desire, to become a black witch or bamboozling sorcerer. My true wish was to obtain clarity and understanding about my path and my existence and, like everyone here, find my actual purpose. After weeks of prayer I decided to try some of these tools. Truthfully, this was the experimental phase of my development, and I tried and played with many tools, of which only a few resonated. Feeling more comfortable, I quickly devoured all the knowledge in this book and cautiously completed a few of the exercises. Surprisingly, I began to feel a bit more comfortable shifting into a new spiritual practice and ideology. I cannot deny that there was a film of residual guilt in my heart and mind; however, in truth, I could not help but feel I was on to something unique, valuable, and oddly familiar.

In *The Psychic Pathway*, I was introduced to the existence of guardian angels and spirit guides or traveling companions.[23] Sonia wrote that we truly did have guardian angels that connected with us at the time of our birth and remained with us throughout our lives to help us complete our life purpose.[24] This concept was not difficult to believe, and I easily accepted it. Of course, since I was familiar with the archangels mentioned in the Bible, I did not doubt their existence or the reality of guardian angels, since it is documented that we were given angels to help us: "[God] *will command his angels concerning you to guard you in all your ways*"[25] and "*Are not all angels ministering spirits sent to serve those who will inherit salvation?*"[26]

Sonia declares that each person on this Earth was gifted a spiritual team, which includes spirit guides.[27] These guides serve as teachers who nudge us in a particular direction and teach us every step of the way, either bringing us joy or helping us reach a level of spiritual growth and evolution. I struggled with this concept. This certainly was news to me. I seriously questioned if God had truly provided us spiritual helpers or invisible assistants throughout our lives.

There were, of course, many times when I wish I could have truly seen one extend a hand to lift me up. This surely was not written as a separate chapter in the Bible. There was no mention of a spirit guide aiding our growth, helping us elevate our consciousness and extend our minds beyond the limitations of this world. I needed definitive proof of this. During my quest for empirical evidence, I read everything I could find online about spirit guides, and it turns out I was completely ignorant. The internet contained so much information about spirit guides, including who they were, how to contact them, and how many we have. So many people already knew their guide and believed they existed. I felt I had missed some critical moment in time, an information age of which I was not privy to. I decided to continue with Sonia's work and studied her book *Ask Your Guides*.[28]

From this little gem, I learned that I had a loving spirit guide who had been with me and supported me throughout my entire lifetime on Earth.[29] This guide has previously incarnated into Earth many times and, through their physical embodiments, spiritually evolved through many incarnations; they only occasionally take physical form for further development. They choose to teach and guide us as we teach them during our very own incarnation.[30] Apparently, we have many guides who walk in and out of our lives to assist us throughout our personal development.

In addition to spirit guides, I learned about the concept of the higher self. I signed up for a one-month meditation course online, with its initial focus on discovering your higher self. The "higher self" is defined as our true presence that guides us every day and always remains connected to the creator. Aligning with our higher self, that part of us that is always with God and retains perfect knowledge of our true identity, enables us to live our true life purpose through love. Our higher self, according to this course, is always accessible and retains an objective perspective, which is invaluable and assists in our personal evolution.

I acknowledge that I was experiencing an internal struggle during this process. First, my mind tried to determine whether any of this was a possibility. Initially I made a logical list of why this could not be true. After all, if this *was* true, why wasn't this mentioned in the Bible? I thought this was incredibly valuable information; why didn't the entire population know this? This was so far removed from my world as a Christian. There were many days I spent contemplating this possibility. After much thought, I prayed for validation and let it go.

I returned to *The Psychic Pathway* and was attracted to the section on automatic writing.[31] Early on, I intentionally avoided this section and refused to try the exercises. However, there was an inner nudge to revisit this section.

Automatic writing, a form of spirit communication, allows your guides, or higher self, to utilize your hand to write.[32] At an early point on my journey, I did not know if spirit guides existed, and I certainly did not know if I wanted to establish communication if it was possible. Indeed, I believed this was another manipulative trick of the Devil. How would I know I was not being deceived? I endured many bouts of paranoia about establishing contact, if that was even within the realm of possibility. Initially, I was terrified of the thought of some other being controlling my hand to write, or to do anything with my body for that matter. Visions of *The Exorcist*, in all of its holy terrifying glory, plagued my mind, and I warned myself that surely would be the outcome. But internally, I was being pushed to try. Make contact. After all, who had spent the past thirty years trying to get my attention? I got on my knees and prayed for help, protection, and clarity. After much doubt and apprehension, I convinced myself to just pick up the pen and try. I repeatedly read about the process to confirm my understanding. While my spirit was moving forward on a pathway of intrigue, mysticism, and light, it still embodied my Christian fear and hesitation.

I finally mustered the courage to try automatic writing a few weeks later. I prayed heavily for protection from what I considered to be the dark empire, and wrote a question on a piece of paper. I sat at my desk and waited for a mystical presence to move my hand. But nothing came. After ten minutes, I gave up. I remembered reading that it could take several tries until it actually happened. While I was not ever one to give up or surrender, I assumed that this was not for me.

Days later, after meditation, I tried again to no avail. I posed a different question every day, hoping for someone to respond, but no one ambulated through the ethers to reply. I shifted my focus toward a variety of meditations and stopped asking questions. The more I meditated, however, the more determined I became to master automatic writing. I wondered why no one wanted to speak to me. Was I really that unworthy, and where were the hounds of Hell? As I was going through this process of spiritual emergence, I was still adapting to living in a new city, and I struggled to become friends with Noah's friends, since I felt we had nothing in common. Instead, I preferred to spend my time alone, as always. This was becoming a major issue between us, and it was a recurring problem in my life. During my tenth attempt at automatic writing, I finally asked why it was that I preferred solitude as opposed to being social. This was deeply affecting my life, and I hoped for some insight. At this time, I posed my question to the universe at large and specified that a benevolent being reply. To my surprise, I heard a low voice speak: "*In a past life, you were a beggar, a thief, and a healer. You were destitute. Because you were a thief, you stole, and were ashamed of what you did, and you did not want to be around anyone. You used your subconscious to heal, and no one wanted to be around you."*

I lay my pen down on my journal to read what I had just written. Oddly enough, I did not feel a sensation in my hand but had clearly heard a voice speak as I wrote. Was this automatic writing? It took a few minutes to digest these words. What did this mean? Did I really just believe what I had written? Did I just make this up? I decided to ask a different question: *Why do I worry all the time, and why am I so fearful?* I paused briefly but could feel pressure in and around my head as the words flowed through me.

You were a loner, and no one was there to help you at all. You had to learn by yourself and guide yourself. You were never sure or certain of what was right or what was wrong—could not discern at all. You were scared of yourself, that you couldn't achieve anything or do anything right. Gave up too early—easily discouraged, fearful, scared, sorrow, sadness, loveless.

Again, I felt no overriding pressure in my hand, I was in full control. This could not be automatic writing. I thought this was just my imagination, and I felt an overwhelming sense of doubt as I read these words aloud. This message implied the existence of past lives, and I had not subscribed to that belief at the time. No one likes to hear that they were loveless and extraordinarily indecisive and unsure. Obviously, I was not impressed by the answer. I gave my ego the full jurisdiction of my mind as I looked for a way to discredit the message. However, at the same time, I wondered if this could possibly be true. I also speculated about who was disseminating this information. I flipped through many metaphysical books to look for explanations about the phenomenon I had experienced.

Upon my search, I came across the spiritual practice called channeling, whose textbook definition matched what I had just experienced. I learned that channeling is a process that allows us to access higher realms and communicate with spirit guides, angels, and other light beings.[33] I wondered if my spirit guide was attempting to communicate with me through channeling, and if so, how was I actually doing this? From my studies of channeling methodologies, I learned that I had to achieve a relaxed state of consciousness but maintain concentration and focus.[34] For those who have already been practicing meditation and concentration and have achieved a relaxed state of mind, the channeling process is relatively easy. Given that my meditations were all about learning to focus and concentrate, I assumed I was being prepared to learn to channel. In an attempt to access higher realms, which include spirit guides and other light beings, it is necessary to shift your attention inward and upward.[35] Regardless of what I was learning, I continued to fear whom I was communing with and their intentions. This mental mile marker on my journey was furnished with an enormous sense of doubt, and my perception of what was real, and what could exist, was beginning to fracture. I was being pushed beyond my limits of what I was willing to believe.

Courageously I continued to practice what I now know as channeling. To protect myself from what I believed were the overlords of the dark dominion, I prayed and asked God and the angels to be with me and guide my learning. I closed my eyes and called out to the celestial beings of light for answers. To be honest, at the time, I wasn't sure exactly whom I was communicating with; I trusted that these beings had good intentions mainly based on the quality of the messages they provided me at the time. At the infancy of our correspondence, my questions ranged from "Why am I here?" to "How do I improve my meditations?" The answers consisted of a few sentences to a small paragraph. I was told, on one occasion, that I needed visualization to improve my meditation. I asked for details and was given the names of two psychics, of whom I was already aware, as suggestions.

In the evening time, I lay in bed reading as much as possible about channeling, meeting spirit guides, and all things encompassing spiritual development. While I was uncertain about the actual existence of spirit guides, I knew I was becoming anxious to meet one if they were real. Recently I learned a technique by Choquette that would help me meet my guide.[36] Per Sonia, I was instructed to ask silently, or aloud, the name of my guide upon falling asleep in bed at night. She further stated that this could be done upon waking.[37] Again, I was paralyzed with fear. What if I asked and some dark voice replied? I knew that before I would even try, I would make Nicole do it first. She was braver working with the occult.

I called her and asked her to try asking for her guide's name before she went to bed, and without fail, she did. To her excitement she heard a small voice speak the name *Virgil*. My sister ranted about the oddity of the name. Truly, I was excited for her, and I wanted to try; however, I was still hesitant and I made my best friend ask the next night. She called me and told me she heard a name, *Hazel*, ringing throughout the bedroom. Excited by this news, I mustered the nerve to ask my guide their name. The next night I lay in bed, closed my eyes, and asked, "What's your name?" I heard nothing. Admittedly, I was disappointed and fell straight to sleep. The following evening I tried again. I asked silently,

"What's your name?" A flood of names filled the room, but I did not trust them. I already believed that the house was haunted, and assumed that it was the disincarnate spirits who were speaking. I fell asleep soon afterward. In the middle of the night, I tossed and turned and heard a small voice murmur, "Orion." Exhausted, I replied, "thank you," and fell back into a deep sleep.

The next morning began like any other. I went running and meditated. Once in the shower I was gently reminded that I had heard a name. My eyes expanded, my heart began to beat very fast, and I rejoiced. I heard it. I *had* heard something. But was I being tricked or was this a good entity? Was God going to teach me a very profound lesson about engaging with the supernatural?

I grabbed my pen and paper that afternoon with every intention of speaking to Orion. Although I really had no clue how to do it, I knew that I could. An acute sense of fear and doubt lurked in the pathways of my mind, and I hesitated putting pen to paper. I clearly remembered the many biblical verses in the book of Leviticus:

If a person turns to mediums and necromancers, whoring after them, I will set my face against that person and will cut him off from among his people.

And,

Do not turn to mediums or necromancers; do not seek them out, and so make yourselves unclean by them: I am the Lord your God."[38]

I prayed before I asked Orion to present himself to me. I put pen to paper and asked him who he was, why he was here, and what he wanted with me.

Shortly thereafter I felt an enormous pressure billow around my head and my body. I also felt nauseated and anxious, which I learned is a common phenomenon among channelers. A voice pierced through the veil and recited the following:

Allow me to introduce myself, I am Orion, the high one, the high priest, the one from above. I have come, or you have chosen me to be your guide and your teacher, as we are all your teachers and you for us as well. Dear one, it has been a pleasure being with you on this long, hard, and arduous journey, although it seems as if we've just begun. Dear one, I am with you always. I watch you while you sleep. I protect your soul, spirit as it migrates out of body to the spirit land. For you dear, I bring messages of love, clarity, and self-forgiveness, all of which are lessons and work, and even you could say that these are assignments chosen by you and selected by us to help you on this great journey here on this planet you call Earth. Dear child, I am delighted to meet you and speak to you formally, although we have had many encounters thus far, but maybe you don't remember them all.

Dear one, it is a pleasure to be in such company today. I am proud to be your guide and helper. The lessons in which I come to help you include the heart, as you've seen in your meditation—for the heart is the most important thing; it is the glue that holds things together; it binds us all and when that is torn or ripped from the Earth, there is only pure chaos ensuing. These things we come here to teach you, and about love, forgiveness. Especially for you dear one, is a lesson of forgiveness and even one of sheer joy and happiness. There is a great change on your planet. Beings are now reaching to the stars for answers, for help, even on the inside, which is where you should look.

If I may, my beautiful one, I am simply a star here to help you go forward into the light of God. I am simply here to aid you or help you on your way, your journey through the stars, back to the great one we call the Jehovah, or as you call him, the holy mother-father God, which is great as he is all that is and that will ever be.

For you ask my role, for I am a guide, but also a teacher as we all have lessons to share and learn. Blessed be. For your gift is truly great. Communion is a blessing; for to talk to the stars and angels is truly a gift from the great one, the love of all love, the source of all sources. Many many blessings, let God be with you.

As I wrote this message, I felt a powerful energy surge through my body. I knew I was consciously capturing and writing the message as the words streamed through my mind; however, I was not fully aware of its significance and power until I stopped to review it. This guide, who called himself Orion, had a bubbly personality and was fundamentally spirited. To be frank, I knew that these words did not emanate from my being. Orion was a real being, and in my heart I felt that he was a real guide and he was mine. I rejoiced that this was real, that he was real.

Awakening the Psychic Self

Every morning I began my day in meditation. I knew that I could hear Orion, but I was determined to meet him face to face. For several days I tried, without success. However, when I asked him why I could not see him, he instructed me to just close my eyes and he would be there. After many attempts, I still could not see him. Days later, he explained that I needed a guided meditation. My online course included meditations to meet my higher self and spirit guide, so I decided to complete them, hoping my guide would appear.

It took many attempts to experience a breakthrough. Finally, and unexpectedly, during a meditation where I was trying to meet my higher self, Orion appeared. In this meditation, I was led to the doors of a big white house with Greek columns, a mix between New World plantation and classical Greek. As I walked in, I explored the rooms of this two-story house, but intuitively I knew I was supposed to walk into the big living room to the left. I could feel my stomach tighten as I took steps around the corner; I wondered who was waiting for me and if I would be safe. My eyes darted around this grand living room. There was a long wooden table in the center of the room, along with an oversized silver mirror on the wall and decadent red paisley chairs. As I explored the room, an old woman appeared. She stood beside a long, blue pine table with a big bushel of peaches. Standing next to her was a younger woman with long blonde hair, who was folding the crust of a pie. She introduced herself as Izzy and asked if I wanted to help make a peach pie.

The elderly woman said nothing but looked at me curiously. She was a very short woman with grayish-blond bangs and long, straight hair running down her shoulders. She wore a long black dress with small, crimped ruffles lying across her chest, which was reminiscent of nineteenth-century garb. Three different necklaces circled this woman's neck. She wore various silver jewelry pieces, including rings and earrings that hung heavily on her small frame. A gypsy woman, I thought. She was so old that I automatically assumed she didn't have any teeth. I responded to the younger woman and agreed to help her. The woman guiding the meditation prompted me to ask my higher self questions, but truthfully I was focused on being in the moment. While I was helping to fold the crust, I noticed someone else sitting in one of the red paisley-printed chairs. I looked over to the left and saw a man, but only from the neck down, clothed in Roman soldier gear. He took his finger in the air and drew symbols for me: a heart and a six-pointed Star of David. I made a mental note of these symbols. Automatically I knew it was Orion. I thanked him and my higher self for being present and walked out of the house as I had been prompted.

Outside the French doors, a cobblestone pathway led to a small flower garden with a large fountain. I was guided to find a gift in the garden, a gift that would help me on my journey. In a small, gray stone cutout, I saw a little wooden box, grabbed it, and opened it. There was a gold bracelet and a key shaped like an ankh. Slowly I brought myself out of the meditation. What an experience! I couldn't wait to ask Orion the meaning behind the symbols he drew for me. I was truly overwhelmed that I had met my higher self and seen my guide, albeit partially!

That same day, I sat down at my dining-room table and prepared myself to speak to Orion. Almost immediately, I felt a cloud of pressure encase my head and I knew that Orion was there. Anxiously, I questioned him about the heart and star that he drew for me in meditation, and of course I thanked him for being there. He explained that the six-pointed star, also known as the Star of David or the Merkaba Star, is a star of connection; as above, so below. The star, he said, is a reminder of my journey, where to look for hope, compassion, love, and forgiveness, which resides within us all, the eternal tank of love that flows over. The heart, he explained, was to remind me to open to love, since love is the strongest force there is.

I made the concerted effort to meet Orion alone in mediation two weeks following this conversation. While I could hear him speak, I still could not meet with him individually. Repeatedly, he instructed me to close my eyes and trust he was there. And each time I was unable to see him. It occurred to me to try to reach Orion in my dream state. While lying down in bed one evening, I asked Orion to appear in my dreams, since I was desperate to see his face. That night, at the tail end of a dream, I sat at the bottom of a staircase with a man whose face was cloudy and fuzzy. He asked me if I was ready to meet him, and I eagerly said yes. He snapped his fingers three times and a voice called my name in the bedroom. My eyes flipped open, and I looked around to see if Noah was awake and needed my help. He was fast asleep. I heard the voice state my name loudly. Again, I was too afraid to respond and buried my face in my pillow and prayed.

The next morning I prayed and meditated to clear my chakras and to prepare myself to channel. As we spoke, Orion told me that it was he who had been calling my name all along, and that for countless years I had been too afraid to speak. He urged me to speak without fear or hesitation. I felt sadness and guilt in my heart after he, a magnificent being of light, had been trying to help me all along throughout my life, and I had allowed my fear to prevent a beautiful gift. As our conversation continued, Orion revealed my natural spiritual abilities that I willed into being prior to my incarnation:

For you ask to be a divine vessel of light, for you already are, you are born this way, we all are. You have a great many gifts and talents, we all do. For you my dear is the gift of sight and sound; for you hear the ethers and the wind in the ethers, these great voices of the mighty ones, the holy ones. Blessed be, for you truly are talented and blessed with a gift of sound, for to hear us is truly a miracle of God, the mighty one. For you hear us all, and even him, the voice of all voices, the mighty one, for he resides inside of you. Blessed be.

While this information was incredibly helpful, I still doubted the level of my potential. There is a big difference between believing and knowing. In this case, I believed that I could hear spirits, but I experienced several moments of doubt; therefore, I did not know for certain.

For months, I practiced meditation and finished my online course, which greatly helped improve my focus and increase my faith in my gifts. My relationship with my guide strengthened as we communicated daily. While he spoke to me in words, he also showed me many symbols. I decided to create my own symbolic dictionary so that I could reference it whenever I needed to. Orion helped me to be honest with myself about my own personal struggles, my lack of self-worth, and my unhappiness, fear, and anxiety. As painful as it was to hear, it was very important to confront my afflictions.

Orion also assisted me in perceiving my circumstances and situations differently, from multiple perspectives, as opposed to just my own. There wasn't a day we did not communicate; he became my elder brother. The nature of our communication changed the more I channeled him. Throughout the day, I could hear Orion speak to me as I contemplated life and hardship, and even as I judged and disapproved of someone's actions.

On one occasion, Noah and I were involved in an intense discussion about God. He and I had very different beliefs about what God was and why we were here. At the end of our heated debate, I heard my guide tell me clearly, "He is not ready yet. Do not force him. Spirit is never forced." This stopped me in my tracks. I promptly ended our discussion and told my boyfriend that I respected his beliefs or lack thereof. A majority of my romantic relationships were with men who claimed atheism as their belief system. I felt that I had to defend my beliefs about God and felt the need to instruct others about what I believed they failed to know or recognize.

This one swift comment by Orion shifted my perception of what I believed the spiritual journey was supposed to entail. I thought that as spiritual Samaritans, it was our duty to dictate what was correct and incorrect regarding someone's spiritual path. I realized this belief carried over from my experiences as a Christian. I recognized that when someone is ready to consciously pursue this type of journey, then they will wholeheartedly seek it. Although this might be a simple lesson for most, it was not one for me. The belief about damnation of the soul, Hellfire, and brimstone was deeply embedded within my psyche, and I wanted to prevent everyone I knew from this, especially Noah.

The month of August was spent completing a draft of my dissertation, meditating, and reading anything related to psychic development. My hunger for spiritual knowledge and the occult was unquenchable. I found myself reading every imaginable book and listening to countless podcasts on spiritual development. The world as I perceived it was changing. As if handed a gift from the sky, I felt that my consciousness was in a state of expansion during my quest for truth.

After my sessions with Orion, I began to wonder about the limitations of my spiritual communication. Did my ability really span the ethers? Could I even speak to the angels? Or what about the archangels? I pondered if God would even allow such things. And as a beautiful response to all my relentless contemplation, the angels answered.

One morning, after I finished my run and meditation, I decided to find a new spiritual podcast. I steadily looked for validation of all that I was experiencing and learning. In one particular podcast, the show's guest discussed how she channeled her angels daily and encouraged listeners to try to communicate with their guardian angels. She further articulated the simple fact that channeling these light beings was easier than it appears. Simply a thought and intention would do. Intuitively I knew this was a green light. I was going to shift my focus toward communicating with the angels and archangels.

Truthfully, I did not know how to begin. Was I supposed to call on them individually by name, and would they appear? I took out my journal where I kept all of Orion's messages, and closed my eyes. I prayed for protection and for the presence of the archangels. I asked my heart for a sincere question. What did I truly want to know? What was the desire of my heart? I opened my heart and asked one of the archangels I was most familiar with, Archangel Michael, what it looked like here to walk the spiritual path as a human.

Humans and source are never separated. They are one in one, one in the same forms of connectedness. You ask, what is it to walk with God while being here? Well, you could ask, what is it like for a fish to be without the sea? Lost, alone, no waters to tread. It cannot survive without the source.

For the source is the life, the breath, the very being of one, or of your life you could say. To walk this path is a somewhat difficult one for you, or at least for humans—too much distance from God, or a sense of forgetfulness, is overwhelming, too much use of the ego, not the source, which lies within all of us. God is the one, the source, the way, the light, and the force. Without him, you cannot be, do not exist. It is through him that you live, breath, walk, and exist.

To walk this path, you must look within, not without, for therein the truth lies. For it always has lied within you and always will. The truth will guide you to your path to walk, on an even path with God. For, of course, there are errors, trials, lessons, for the soul came here to experience all of these, which you as a spirit or soul make manifest; for therein lies the truth of your being here, for a temporary time at least.

For you, Deanna, this path is a difficult or hard one, but one lit with the flame of the lord, the god source, or as you say, the holy mother-father god source. For you seek truth always, you always have. For it is in you where the flame of God burns deeply and brightly, for your love of him is not lost and never has been. But, please remember that the truth, or God's truth, sets you free; your freedom from deep-seated fear, your angst or anxiety. Without God, these can perpetuate, but with God, these chords will be severed, and you will fly like a bird alongside the flame of God. For it is within you to walk the spiritual path of God. For he resides inside of you. He loves you and never gives up on you, for this is not even a concept. This is man or human made. For it is only to love that is holy, or God's work, and this too constitutes the spiritual path to walk beside him.

Truth is what you seek. You spend day in and day out to seek this, but it lies within you; follow it and you will be shown all of the great treasures of God. For as you know, and as you seek, these are not material treasures. For those are only treasures of this world, which man has made. We do not call these true treasures. For the treasures of God outweigh the treasures of man and these are the treasures of love, commitment, and devotion to your spirit. For it is the light of the spirit that lifts you into spiritual realms; the lighter the spirit, the less dense the soul. Denseness is almost akin to madness, disconnection from God you could say.

Every being contains a speck of light that shines bright for the truth of God. For it is he who exists and because of him, you exist as co-creators on this great planet by God. For this planet to revolve, it is but the breath of God pushing it round and round like a merry-go-round, but only with his breath. To exist on this planet is to exist in a different format, a physical one to try out new experiences so that you could learn lessons that you couldn't otherwise learn, let's say, in a different dimension. For this is truly special, but it is a difficult and challenging one. To channel this information from us is also truly special and blessed be those who hear this, for these are words of love and the love of God. This is a truly special gift from the one high source.

You ask again, how do I walk this spiritual path? What does it look like? For us in Heaven, it does not look like what you perceive or expect. We have no so-called expectations. We want you to be happy, enjoy your adventure. Enjoy your gift, for it is a gift from God. Fear not, for I am with you on this miraculous journey of love. To walk this path, which is truly a path of love, dear one, is to walk with fearlessness, surety, certainty, love, forgiveness, and gaiety. Be certain that these are descriptions of love and emanate from the light source, from the one true God. For you to walk this path, the God path, you must forgive yourself first to have an open heart. For God is with you, above you, below you, all around he is there. That is all for now.

As I wrote these words I understood the power they carried within my soul. From this message alone, I felt the love of my creator and the expansion of my heart.

I communed with the archangels and my guide daily. While I tuned in, I felt an overwhelming sense of comfort, love, happiness, support, and great wisdom ringing throughout my being. I felt incredibly humbled by this ability. As a naturally curious person, I had many questions, and the angels were amazingly available, patient, and loving. They provided me an insightful objective perspective as a response to my incessant questions, and I felt I had a personal gateway to the unknown. As I channeled these messages, I began to wonder how common this phenomenon was. How many people on this planet were in open communication with the divine? I wondered what had shifted on this Earth plane to allow such ease of access. I asked the archangels to kindly speak about this topic:

Dear one, it is a pleasure to speak with you again this fine day. Blessed be the almighty one. For you ask, what changes are happening on the planet or what vibrations are now present upon this Earth plane you now inhabit? For there are many. A new dawn, a new kingdom is upon you who inhabit the physical plane at the moment. It is a time for change in this world, for pure love to reign this physical plane in which you inhabit. For it is a time for change amongst the people or humans that are inhabiting this place. Much strife, warfare, sadness, for it will soon be a new dawn. A time will come to rejoice in the love and glory of the lord thy God. For it is here that you will feel these changes in a physical sense. You will feel physical changes in the body and mind, which will be most open to messages of the lord. Trust in the lord. For it is a time to rejoice the coming of the lord thy God.

You ask, how will this happen? Well, the vibrational patterns will change upon the Earth into a higher realm, a new dimension. Further, there will be a shift in divine thought. A change will occur in what you as humans call rational thought. For you ask, why at this time on Earth? For it is a period of great change on the Earth, a period to receive. A great awakening has fallen upon the Earth and this will soon manifest upon everyone. The lord thy god is great. Blessed be those who hear this message of God, for God is with you. For you ask, why now? Why this point in time? This time has simply to awaken to the spirit, to the one true god, the great almighty source. For you, too, are experiencing this great awakening. You as well come, or serve, to witness the great divine messages of the lord's work. Blessed be him who lives at this great time. It is a great time for awakening on this planet. Blessed Be, that is all.

For weeks I communed with the angels, archangels, and my spirit guides. Over the course of our channeling sessions, I began to notice changes in my body. Although I ran religiously, I gained weight. My face broke out in severe acne, which was incredibly difficult to control. Some nights I experienced great bouts of insomnia, and other nights I felt I could sleep until my death. Additionally, I experienced periodic cycles of fevers and body aches over many months. The fevers lasted for two days and then my body resumed its natural temperature.

During one alarming episode throughout this process, I attempted to blow-dry my hair; I plugged the chord into the socket and flipped the switch. Within five or six minutes, a massive flame erupted out of the mouth of the hairdryer. It slipped out of my hands onto the floor, and I pulled the plug out of the socket.

Initially, this incident did not concern me, until another jarring event occurred in a similar fashion. While working on my dissertation one afternoon, smoke spewed out of my laptop after I had been using it for only ten minutes. All my electronics were dying upon contact. My flatiron even sparked when I touched it. Something within me was changing, or I was experiencing a cycle of bad luck, which I definitely did not believe in. Concerned, I sat down to research this phenomenon and spent many hours reviewing websites on electrical power surges upon physical touch. As with much internet information, it was my job to filter out all the garbage in the hope of finding a kernel of truth and an experience that paralleled my own.

What I found was a compendium of symptoms that others, like myself, were experiencing. These can be called ascension symptoms.[39] These include but are not limited to flu-like symptoms (achy body, exhaustion, high temperature, insomnia), dizziness, vibration of the body, ringing in the ears, acne, headaches, forgetfulness, and disorientation. While I experienced a majority of these symptoms intermittently over several weeks, it was more challenging to locate a person with similar physical reactions. I prayed and asked for clarity. Was my body truly undergoing an electrical rewiring? Were my experiences a product of the ascension process? I called upon my guide for clarification:

Dear one, for it is I, Orion, come here to help you. You ask, what is wrong with me? Why do I feel sick? Dear one, for you are going through a transformation, a change, a physical one. You ask, why do I feel so sick, so hot? For dear one, you are going through a godly change, an Earthly change. For you ask, why am I experiencing this? Dear one, you ask, why? Why now? For we tell you, you are in service to the lord, to the God source. Dear one, for this requires changes, a great change of heart, body, soul, and spirit, for you are experiencing a change of all of these and a change of the body. You ask, why specifically? Changes are upon you dear one on this Earthly plane. You ask to be of service to the lord thy god. These changes come to you from him, the lord God, for you to serve him on this Earthly plane.

Great changes are upon us here. For this is part of your charge, for these great changes are required to be of service to the great one. Fear not, for God is with you dear one. For you ask if you are sick, why no, this is surely not the case. These are changes required of the body to transmit energy of the high one above here on the Earth plane. Fear not, dear one, for the lord thy God is with you on this day to help you out, to make a great change. Great

61

changes are upon us all. For it is time for a calling, dear one, to the great one above; time for a calling to be of service to the lord, for this requires great changes in your life, which are upon you. So dear one, fear not. That is all.

For even more clarification, I asked the archangels to expand on this concept of ascension.

You are feeling the effects of the ascension process: dizziness, tiredness, exhaustion, unsettledness, even nausea and pain of the body. All of these are maladies necessary for the ascension process. Ascension is a process of growth and change in vibration.

These months were filled with wonder, happiness, frustration, joy, and incredible impatience. My appetite for knowledge was insatiable as I continued to spiritually develop. My mind wanted answers to questions that I had posed throughout my short duration on this planet. In the midst of this, my dissertation became a thorn in my side. As I connected to my guide on a daily basis, I knew I was not going to pursue a career in academia. That career path did not feed my soul, nor did it bring me joy. My soul longed for a new state of being, one where I could be of spiritual service.

Truthfully, my heart desired to be a useful vessel for God. While at that time I could not necessarily articulate what that meant specifically, I embodied that feeling and knowingness. I found myself more often than not on my knees in perpetual states of gratitude. From a worldly perspective, it would appear that I was sacrificing my PhD to be a servant of God. But my heart actually felt a release of pressure, strain, overwhelming anxiety, and palpable fear. I remember hearing from a particular professor who snidely remarked, "What else can you do if you don't do archaeology?" That was not my fear at that time. Although that may have conveyed a message of carelessness to those around me, I was not worried. I was consciously aware of a light burning inside of me so deep and so bright that it was erupting at the surface. I was joyful, and every day brought with it a beautiful message and a deeper commitment to trusting that which lay within me.

Now, do not be mistaken. This is a true process. This internal phenomenon did not appear overnight. For years, I battled myself, my image, my heart, and my mind, as we all do, and I became subservient to my psyche. My ego reminded me daily that I wasn't good enough. I was incapable of competing and succeeding in academia. Who did I think I was? I did not deserve to accomplish my heart's desire. Every day was a personal Hell of which I was the gatekeeper. It was tragic, and I internally crafted a world of solitude and sadness.

As the years passed, I asked myself, What the Hell was I trying to prove, and to whom? Honestly, I did not doubt my capacity to "succeed" at whatever my heart wanted, but did my heart want this exactly? Everyone I knew expected me to become a professor, a great title to share with other friends, and I wanted to teach, but my spirit yearned to learn and teach something else.

I continued to meditate diligently every day. One of the best rewards of my devoted practice was meeting my guardian angels, Haniel and Michael. They disclosed that they have been with me since my incarnation and will be until I depart. They, too, serve as my guides and teachers. As such, they emphasized the importance of daily meditation, or silencing the mind, to listen and focus, as well as prayer and study. My daily practice consisted of grounding and protecting myself, opening and clearing my chakras, and consciously connecting to source. This daily practice brought with it insight about my thoughts and actions, and I was shown self-defeating attributes that I'd developed throughout my life. Initially, I had an excuse for them all.

My parents divorced when I very young. I grew up without my mother. My father resented me. I was ugly and dumb. I allowed people to use me because I was never good enough for anything else. The list goes on and on. I was shown and told to take accountability for my actions, or lack thereof, and for my negative thoughts. I needed to truly release this belief of victimhood. Why is it that what we despise the most we hold on to so tightly? How has our anger, frustration, sadness, and anxiety become our source of comfort? Why are we so in love with our suffering? In the stillness of my mind, I could not hide, and the truth was revealed. My ego was offended and hurt. But my heart cried for freedom and sought to release the self-imposed chains that bound me.

Within a few months of channeling, I firmly decided against pursuing an academic position. That truly was my most freeing thought at the time. I did not feel as if I had anything to prove anymore. It was time to work on self-love and self-acceptance, which encompassed following the desires and passions of my heart and accepting my abilities, bestowed to me by God. Every page I wrote in my dissertation was one day closer to the end of that chapter in my life.

I spent every day listening to messages from the divine source. It was during this communion where I truly felt "home." There was no sense of judgment, fear, pain, or confusion. In my heart, this is where I *always* wanted to be. Although I had spent seven years completing my MA and PhD, I made the decision that I wanted to be at least a part-time channeler to provide messages to those in need. I sat down every morning to ask the archangels for a daily message for my closest friends and family; however, on one particular day, I experienced a very intense conversation that would set the course for my new path.

Dear one, for it is a pleasure to speak to you today, for these are messages from the divine dear one. For fear not, the lord thy god is with you, around you, below you. You ask, what are the messages today? Well, dear one, for these messages are of eternal love, peace, and happiness—for we ask, what makes thou happy? This question seems on the surface to be a simple question, but this is truly not so. What maketh thou happy? To serve the lord thy god? To be at home and at peace, to be one with the lord thy God? What maketh thou happy? For we ask this question for you to contemplate for your life.

Why does thou speak to the above as if thou are separated from source, for no one is separated from source dear one. Why does thou contemplate separation from source, for we are all connected to the lord thy god. To be of the lord thy god is to be happy dear one. For happiness comes like a flame, a bright flame that is akin to the love of God, bright, burning hot—these feelings are the feelings of the source, the lord thy god dear one. We ask, what maketh thou happy? To serve God dear one? What maketh thou happy, for we ask this for a reason. What is your motive for speaking to us day in and day out as if we are not there, as if we are separated from the lord thy god, we are all one dear one. We are all of the lord thy god.

The tone and content of this message was unexpected. I was not sure how to react or what to think. Had I offended them? Was I abusing my ability? I became angry and defensive.

Dear one, for these are messages of the divine. Do not be grieved or angry. We ask truly out of love and concern for you. For we ask, dear one, what do you intend to do with these messages? For we are honored to speak to you dear one. We ask what you intend to do so that we may deliver clearer messages to those in need. This is not to say that you should not speak to us, for it is an honor for us to communicate. For whom else do you intend to send messages? We ask this to provide clearer messages for you and your family.

Dear one, do not be upset. For we ask because we are concerned about your wellbeing and your motives. We wish to help in any way possible, for you ask for messages from the divine. These are messages intended for you and your loved ones. Do not be upset dear one, for we are only concerned for your wellbeing. For we ask, what truly makes you happy? Is it truly to serve God, to be his messenger? We ask so that we may know what messages to deliver. More specifically, do you truly wish to serve the lord thy god? How so? By delivering messages daily to family and friends? By listening to us and the true nature of your heart dear one? We think you should think about this truly and deeply.

I initially responded with confusion. I felt the need to defend myself and my intentions. Did they think I was doing this to praise myself? I did not know what to say. I was so perplexed because of the tone of the message and could not hide my sorrow. I did not expect this type of response that day, or ever, to be honest.

Do not be upset or angry. For we ask because we truly want to know. Only you know what you came here to do or what you truly want to do. To serve the lord thy god requires an open heart, for you truly have this and shall succeed at this. We ask to know so that we may communicate better, so that we may know what tasks are at hand for you. For we truly wish to know what makes you happy? Does serving the lord thy god make you happy dear one? For we ask so that we may make a path for you, a straight path directly to the god source, so that you may serve him directly dear one. For these are messages of the divine. Do not fear, we ask to know so that you will be lifted up into his realm to serve him directly—is this what you wish?

Dear one, we wish to know the true nature of your heart. You ask, are you doing something wrong? Why no, this is not the case. We wish to know if you truly intend to serve the lord thy god. Yes, it has been made clear that you are here to serve him, as we all are, but we wish to know what do you intend to do?

Dear one, we are not upset with you, do not fear. We truly ask so that we may know how to help you. We ask, how do you intend to serve God? By giving messages to loved ones? How far will thou take these messages? We truly ask to help you on your way. Relax, all is well. We wish to help you. We wish to help you back to God or deliver messages from God to those in

65

need. We merely wish to help you, not chastise you. We see that we, God and your spirit guides, make you truly happy. We wish to know how would you like to serve God specifically? By delivering messages? Are there other means that interest you? Please be specific dear one.

I explained to the archangels that I was interested in multiple things and had not yet quite decided.

Well dear one, there are many things you wish to do. Healing is a true task and gift of which you too possess. You wish to help those in need. For this you already do. You give of the heart and hand dear one of your own volition, we know this; you wish to help on another level, this can be done with great diligence, trial, and error. We are here to help you.

In my heart, I knew how much joy I experienced with channeling and giving messages. I saw the profound impact it was having in the lives of the people I knew. Part of me wanted to continue to do this. But I also longed for more. I was genuinely worried that I had greatly offended the angels and was also concerned about how they viewed me and my intentions.

For you wonder, what am I to do? Are the angels mad at me? For surely you know this is not the case dear one. We wish to help you on your way back or path back to God. For you wonder, what am I to do then? Dear one, we are not upset with you or at you, for you wonder is it ok to continue sending messages? Why yes! We think this is a great idea. You wonder what am I to do or what have I done wrong? Well dear one, nothing is wrong in the eyes of God. You wish to continue sending messages. Why, we think this should be so, but take caution and ask why you do this. Be clear with us and to yourself. Is this for praise of self or the lord thy God? Ask yourself truly. For we think it is both, but take caution and heed thy heart dear one. We truly ask, what do you intend to do with your gift? For we think there is much work to be done here on the Earth plane.

For we simply ask, what does thou want to do? Do you want to serve God and help people? Always take heed of thy heart. We know you love him, the lord thy god, and we do know you wish to serve him. We just want to know what else you wish to do? Your destiny is set, but you also have free will to decide your strengths here on this Earth plane. Do you wish to see or hear only or see and hear? These are both important and must be clarified to us. Dear one, we mean to say to you that we must know your true intent dear one, to show this to the true one, the great intent to work with him directly— for there are those of you who wish to serve God directly, more so than others, for we wish to know to what degree? We simply ask how you would like to do this? By what medium dear one? We mean through channeling, sight, seeing, hearing, touching and feeling or by the way of the Tarot? For all of these are great in the eyes of God.

I told the archangels that I wanted to be a channeler and Tarot reader. They replied:

So shall it be. Glory to God in the highest dear one. So it shall be. Blessed be dear one, blessed be. That is all.

I spent my days slowly learning how to read the Tarot and channeling the angels. Although I lacked the ability to see them, their dress, and their faces, I could hear them clearly and later see them as blue, white, and gold sparks. Like many other people, I had endless questions about life, death, reincarnation, karma, sin, Heaven, and Hell. The angels and archangels were accommodating and patient and answered all my questions.

While channeling was the primary way in which we communicated, the angels began to send messages through other mediums; namely, through numbers and other symbols. There is a global experience now known as the 11:11 phenomenon, which is commonly defined as a direct message from the angelic realm, or as an invitation to a celestial gateway.[40] A number of people around the world report frequently seeing 11:11 on their watches, license plates, and phones. While some choose to disregard this message, others have tuned in to research the possible explanation. I was one of those who chose to search, and I found an abundant index of unusual individual experiences citing 11:11.

At the beginning of my exploration, I found a variety of possible meanings. I knew that in numerology, the number 11 was a "master" number, signifying illumination and enlightenment. Others wrote that 11:11 was a global wake-up call, the opening of a spiritual gateway, or a collective awakening for those to fulfill their divine mission on Earth.[41] I began to see 11:11 a month after my first channeling session. This "gateway" appeared everywhere, every day. While I was running, 11:11 appeared in big block letters on billboards, on license plates, and on my watch. I acknowledged it as a door opening for me.

Truthfully, I was not sure what was on the other side of that door, but I was happy to run through it. Eventually, a completely new set of numbers began to occupy my visual frequency. Although 9:11 was still a regular on the dashboard, I became a witness to 111, 222, 333, and 444. The angels were speaking to me through numbers, and I am positive that they led me to Doreen Virtue's book, *Angel Numbers*, in which she defines each number sequence from the angels.[42] While I produced the chapters to my dissertation, I lovingly saw these messages and felt completely supported!

Although most of my channeled messages were geared toward answering life's most-pressing questions, I began to wonder about the limitations of my questioning. Were there any questions that I couldn't ask? Was there information that I was not privy to? My curiosity naturally involved my own growth and spiritual progression. When I first started connecting with my guides and angels, I was told from which lifetime some of my current traits and attributes derived. I prodded further about my past lives and the connections and relationships I had in my current life. Like the other channeling sessions, I prayed, grounded myself, surrounded myself in a bubble of protection, cleared my chakras, and tuned in to the angels for answers about some of my previous lives here in the third dimension. What I experienced was a series of startling revelations about my previous identities and beliefs. I have to admit, there were points during our session when I could not stomach who I had been or accept my actions here on Earth. I felt sad for the old me, and guilt for those I hurt. I learned about my deep connections and karmic entanglements with my father, my sisters, and a few of my friends. The stories that unfolded were beautiful, harsh, sad, and uplifting. As I personally came to learn, I had known my father, sister, and best friend many times throughout the ages, and we had played a variety of roles for different reasons, but with the main goal of spiritual growth.

As I shared this information with my family and friends, they asked if I could obtain information about their previous lives. Without hesitation, I asked for permission to access this information. I have read before about how people carry specific fears acquired from previous lifetimes, including the fear of heights and flying, among many others. Many have come to find the root of their fears through past-life regression, and this process has helped people release fears in their current lifetime. I hoped the information that was channeled through me would help my friends and family as well.

CHAPTER 5

Life after Death

Most people fear death, and many Christians fear the terror of Hellfire and brimstone they'll confront after death, pending their decision to do the "Devil's work," or "psychic work." This idea of a Hellish punishment is predicated on a deeply rooted Christian belief about the nature of psychic practice and God's role as judge, jury, and executioner after death. As detailed in the Bible, sorcerers, also recognized as mediums and psychics, are not allowed to inherit the kingdom of God and unarguably will burn in the lake of fire.[1] These canonical promises are guaranteed to frighten anyone and thus prevent them from even seeking new avenues of thought or ways of believing, and this fear even discourages anyone from using their spiritual gifts. This uncompromising idea about Hell continues to plague current and former Christians. Although there have been numerous documented near-death experiences, channeled messages from the beyond and hypnotherapy sessions, all of which have presented an alternate reality of the afterlife, the enduring belief of Hell continues to dominate the narrative of the Christian afterlife. This persistent belief precludes people from moving forward or even seeking the psychic path.

My hope is to redress this fear about Hell by providing you with an alternative perception of life after death. This is not meant to be a comprehensive dissertation on the afterlife, but a very small thesis on a few of the magically similar life-after-death encounters, along with channeled messages, hypnotherapy sessions, and my own knowledge relayed to me from otherworldly beings of light. First, I must quickly summarize what the Bible reports about death and the afterlife.

Death and Departure

In the Bible, we find that the experience of death is equated to a state of sleep. In the book of Daniel, the phenomenon of the resurrection is annunciated after a period of sleeping in the Earth:

And many of them sleep in the dust of the Earth shall awake, some to everlasting life, and some to shame and everlasting contempt.[2]

Again in the book of Job is the notion of death equated to sleep:

Now shall I sleep in the dust and thou shalt seek me in the morning but I shall not be.[3]

Moreover, this is reiterated in the book of Isaiah:

Your dead ones will live. A corpse of mine—they will rise up. Awake and cry out joyfully, you resident in the dust![4]

Therefore meaning, once we die we simply fall asleep, waiting to awaken in our physical bodies during the second coming. This statement implies that we are composed only of flesh and bone, and because we are only sleeping, we do not experience an afterlife.

In the New Testament, the apostle Paul states that humans are not solely composed of a physical body, but also of a spiritual body, which contradicts earlier passages in the Bible. In the book of 1 Corinthians it is stated:

But some man will say, How are the dead raised up? and with what body do they come? . . . But God giveth it a body as it hath pleased him, and to every seed his own body . . . There are also celestial bodies, and bodies terrestrial: but the glory of the celestial is one, and the glory of the terrestrial is another . . . So also is the resurrection of the dead . . . It is sown a natural body; it is raised a spiritual body. There is a natural body, and there is a spiritual body . . . Howbeit that was not first which is spiritual, but that which is natural; and afterward that which is spiritual . . . And as we have borne the image of the Earthy, we shall also bear the image of the Heavenly. Now this I say, brethren, that flesh and blood cannot inherit the kingdom of God; neither doth corruption inherit incorruption.[5]

This begs the question, If the physical body is "asleep," what happens to the spiritual body? In the book of Ecclesiastes it is written: "*Then shall the dust return to the Earth as it was: and the spirit shall return unto God who gave it.*"[6] In Genesis it is stated that man is formed from the dust of the ground, and his soul is placed within the body or animates the body only once God breathes life into man: "*And the LORD God formed man of the dust of the ground, and breathed into his nostrils the breath of life; and man became a living soul.*"[7] In Job, man's physical body is again referred to as dust.[8] Once the physical body returns to the Earth, the spirit returns to God.

It is not disclosed in the Bible if the spiritual journey home is an immediate or extended process. Documented in Ecclesiastes is the revelation of the silver cord, which allows the spirit body to stay attached to the physical body: "*Or ever the silver cord be loosed, or the golden bowl be broken, or the pitcher be broken at the fountain, or the wheel broken at the cistern.*"[9]

In the scripture, the golden bowl, pitcher, and wheel are metaphors for life. Being broken, they are no longer able to perform their function. This is the same for the physical body—when its purpose has been fulfilled, the vessel will be disbanded. As noted in Ecclesiastes, once this cord is severed, the spirit body will detach to return to God.

The only statement in the Bible about the actual journey back to God is in Psalms: "*Yea, though I walk through the valley of the shadow of death, I will fear no evil: for thou art with me; thy rod and thy staff they comfort me.*"[10] This valley is commonly understood and accepted as the shadowy threshold we traverse after death. What awaits us after this mini sojourn? There is a common reference about seeing the light at the end of the tunnel; does this truly happen, and if so, why isn't it mentioned in the Bible? We are only told through Jesus as he addressed his disciples in I John: "*In my Father's house are many mansions: if it were not so, I would have told you. I go to prepare a place for you.*"[11] In some Christian denominations this statement is accepted as a literal interpretation, whereby after death we travel to an actual abode where the spirit resides in Heaven.

Heaven

What does the Bible reveal about Heaven? Is this the land of milk and honey and cherubs and harps conventionally depicted in movies and books? The apostle Paul tells us that after death we will be "*away from the body and at home with the Lord.*"[12] While on the cross, Jesus tells the crucified thief immediately before his death: "*Truly I say to you, today you will be with me in Paradise.*"[13] This implies that the thief would be traveling to an afterlife called Paradise upon his death. Heaven is traditionally understood as being the Paradise repeatedly referenced in the Bible. Further, we learn that the majesty of Heaven is humanly indescribable: "*What no eye has seen, what no ear has heard, and what no human mind has conceived— the things God has prepared for those.*"[14] In Ephesians, we are told that in Heaven: "*there might be demonstrated the incomparable riches of his undeserved kindness in his graciousness toward us.*"[15] It is commonly accepted that only the righteous enter Heaven or the kingdom of God.

Hell

Hell, as relayed in the Bible, was originally designed for Satan and his followers as a place of punishment and torment for their transgressions against God. However, these are not Hell's only inhabitants. Hell is also reserved for the wicked, sorcerers, and mediums, and for those who do not believe in, and reject, Jesus the Christ. This is clearly conveyed in the prophetic book of Revelation: "*But the cowardly, the unbelieving, the vile, the murderers, the sexually immoral, those who practice magic arts, the idolaters and all liars—they will be consigned to the fiery lake of burning sulfur. This is the second death.*"[16]

Hell is also mentioned in the book of Mark:

And if thy hand offend thee, cut it off: it is better for thee to enter into life maimed, than having two hands to go into Hell, into the fire that never shall be quenched.[17]

Where their worm dieth not, and the fire is not quenched. For everyone shall be salted with fire, and every sacrifice shall be salted with salt.[18]

It is further reiterated as a fiery place in Matthew: "*You fool! Shall be in danger of the fire of Gehenna.*"[19] In the New Testament, Jesus repeatedly speaks of Hell, which he refers to as Gehenna. While Gehenna in various Christian Bibles is translated as "Hell," it was likely referring to the Valley of Hinnom, a place, prior to the birth of Jesus, that worshiped Molech, represented by the golden calf.[20] This religion of Canaan was reformed under King Josiah, and during the life of Jesus this valley became a dumping ground where garbage was burned. In Matthew, Jesus describes Hell as a fiery furnace: "*The Son of man shall send forth his angels, and they shall gather out of his kingdom all things that offend, and them which do iniquity; And shall cast them into a furnace of fire: there shall be wailing and gnashing of teeth.*"[21]

After the "last judgment," it is decided where the sinful sons of man will spend their eternal resting place. Documented throughout the Bible, but more so in the New Testament, is the final judgment of each individual on the Earth based upon their actions. It is clearly expressed in the book of John: "*Do not marvel at this; for the hour is coming in which all who are in graves will hear his voice and come forth—those who have done good, to the resurrection of life, and those who have done evil, to the resurrection of condemnation.*"[22]

Again, in the books of Romans and Revelation, the dead are awakened to face their last judgment according to their deeds. Romans: [*God*] "*will give to each person according to what he has done.*"[23] Revelation:

> *Then I saw a great white throne and him who sat on it, from whose face the Earth and the Heaven fled away. And here was found no place for them. And I saw the dead, small and great. And another book was opened, which is the Book of Life: And the dead were judged out of those things, which were written in books, according to their works.*[24]

As part of the second death, the wicked are then cast into a lake of fire, as documented in Revelation: "*The sea gave up the dead that were in it, and death, and Hades gave up the dead that were in them, and each person was judged according to what they had done. Then death and Hades were thrown into the lake of fire. The lake of fire is the second death.*"[25]

For the unrighteous, Hell is eternal: "*And these will go away, into eternal punishment, but the righteous into eternal life.*"[26] This is reiterated in the book of Revelation: "*the smoke of their torment goes up forever and ever, and they have no rest day or night.*"[27]

The Second Coming

As revealed in Revelation, holy and righteous Christians will be resurrected and reign with Christ on Earth during the 1,000 years of peace initiated by Christ upon his return:

> And I saw thrones, and they sat upon them, and judgment was given unto them: and I saw the souls of them that were beheaded for the witness of Jesus, and for the word of God, and which had not worshipped the beast, neither his image, neither had received his mark upon their foreheads, or in their hands; and they lived and reigned with Christ a thousand years. But the rest of the dead lived not again until the thousand years were finished. This is the first resurrection. Blessed and holy is he that hath part in the first resurrection: on such the second death hath no power, but they shall be priests of God and of Christ, and shall reign with him a thousand years.[28]

The dead will essentially awaken to a new Earth, as documented in Isaiah: "*For, behold, I create new Heavens and a new Earth: and the former shall not be remembered, nor come into mind.*"[29]

Subsequently, after this period of peace, the Devil will be released from his prison, and a battle will occur between the righteous and the holy ones, as reported in Revelation:

> And I stood upon the sand of the sea, and saw a beast rise up out of the sea, having seven heads and ten horns, and upon his horns ten crowns, and upon his heads the name of blasphemy. And the beast which I saw was like unto a leopard, and his feet were as the feet of a bear, and his mouth as the mouth of a lion: and the dragon gave him his power, and his seat, and great authority . . . And they worshipped the dragon which gave power unto the beast: and they worshipped the beast, saying, Who is like unto the beast? Who is able to make war with him? And there was given unto him a mouth speaking great things and blasphemies; and power was given unto him to continue forty and two months . . . And it was given unto him to make war with the saints, and to overcome them: and power was given him over all kindreds, and tongues, and nations. And all that dwell upon the Earth shall worship him, whose names are not written in the book of life of the Lamb slain from the foundation of the world.[30]

The defeat of Satan follows shortly thereafter. At some point, there is a resurrection of the wicked, or those who carry the mark of the beast, to face their last judgment. In John it is written:

Marvel not at this: for the hour is coming, in the which all that are in the graves shall hear his voice, and shall come forth; they that have done good, unto the resurrection of life; and they that have done evil, unto the resurrection of damnation.[31]

These souls are then condemned to the lake of fire as the second death.

Those spirits who acted faithfully as servants of Christ are rewarded with eternal life. I must emphasize here that there are variations of Christ's second coming due to diverse interpretations between religious denominations. There are many contradictions and points of confusion regarding death, the afterlife, the second coming, and Heaven and Hell. For one, there is no mention of the spiritual body in the second coming of Christ; rather, there is an emphasis on the corporeal or Earthly vessel. Second, and notably, how can the valley of the shadow of death be reconciled with the idea that we sleep in the dust after death? Moreover, for the righteously resurrected, where are they spending their eternal lives? In Paradise or upon the newly created Earth? Are we to assume this is one and the same? These are only a few areas of inquiry. The process of death and the afterlife is not decidedly clear in the Bible and, again, is subject to the interpretation of one's faith and denomination.

While many in the New Age community have completely eschewed the messages of the Bible, there are some striking parallels between the content in the Bible and that from near-death experiences (or NDEs), channeled messages, and sessions from past-life and life-between-life regressions. I will now review what I find to be a few of the most detailed works on life after death from NDEs, channeled works, and hypnotherapy sessions.

Death and Departure

At the outset I want to make clear that NDEs vary in their content, which is to be expected. You will find, however, compelling similarities in a majority of NDE accounts in regard to the physical dying process. One common experience involves the business of being dislodged from the body. It is frequently noted in several NDEs that upon death, a person experiences a floating sensation, usually a detachment from the body. This phenomenon can be defined as the soul's separation from its host. For some, the recognition is swift, but for others, there is a gradual awareness and understanding that they no longer have a physical embodiment. In one notable NDE, documented by Betty J. Eadie in *Embraced by the Light*, she describes this detachment from the body as a magnetic force releasing her from her chest, extracting the soul upward out of the body.[32] Some people who have had NDEs report seeing the presence of a cord as they disconnect from the body. This cord, connecting the spirit and the body, is described as being silver or gray. From these NDEs, we learn that this cord has its parallel in the material world. The physical correlate is a mother's umbilical cord, which is attached to her baby and then is severed to experience the human sensations of life here on Earth.[33] When this silver cord is severed, the spirit is free to transition into the spirit world to experience life as a spirit without its physical embodiment. The location of this cord varies among NDE accounts. A number of accounts report that the silver cord is connected to the abdomen, the back, or the top of the head, or to the feet and even the chest.[34] Some individuals express a simple transition forward without having seen this cord at all.

As told in a few NDEs from Dr. Raymond Moody's research presented in *Life after Life*, many patients have described being pulled by a strong gravitational force into an area of darkness, a dark void, or the "tunnel" as it is popularly understood.[35] In some instances, people report not having crossed a tunnel of darkness, but instead instantly witness the appearance of a light that eventually forms into an angel, a family member, a guide, or a popular religious figure such as Jesus. This religious figure lovingly guides the person through a life review, highlighting important and minor moments to understand their successes and their shortcomings or missed opportunities. There are variations of this experience and its purpose. For example, in Eadie's NDE, she discloses that Jesus, with his golden halo and luminescent light, came to greet her after her travel through the dark tunnel.[36]

In other accounts, individuals report confusion upon physical detachment. They are left for a short period of time to roam, trying to comprehend their new situation.[37] In those reports, individuals conclude that it is the true acceptance and awareness of their "death" that summons the light being. From there, some individuals are then carried to a few realms of Heaven. A majority of NDEs lack such an extensive narrative, however, or at least the person does not remember being taken anywhere. In Eadie's account, she details her journey to what she calls the library of the mind, where all knowledge of the universe is housed and obtainable.[38]

In George Ritchie's NDE, documented in *Return from Tomorrow*, he describes encountering university-like realms dedicated to varied forms of study, as well as music halls and a library. In channeled works, we find similar elements of the afterlife.[39] I am hesitant to call this the Heaven noted in the Bible, but it very well may be. The late psychic Sylvia Browne noted that there are halls of records, charts, research, justice, and wisdom, along with temples dedicated to healing, penance, learning, and voices.[40] In hypnotherapy sessions, we find parallel instances of individuals being taken to or spending their time in libraries or the hall of records, studying their past-life mistakes and successes.

For those with a more extensive sojourn in the afterlife, we find that death is an experience of perfect love, even during the life review. Those individuals who encountered their religious teacher, such as Jesus, report that it was not an experience of judgment or condemnation, but rather one of love and understanding. Some NDEs return to Earth with a new mission or some grand life-altering epiphany regarding their life purpose. I think it is important to mention here two separate experiences whereby NDEs provide explanations about why we are here and further expound on the interconnectedness of all things.

Similar to many NDEs, Ritchie eventually encounters Jesus, who presents him with a life review and then poses the following question: "What did you do with your life?"[41] Initially thinking that Jesus was referencing his achievements in life, Ritchie declares all of his early life successes. He quickly finds that Jesus was referencing his treatment of others as being the most important thing while on Earth. From his pilgrimage into death, we learn that giving love is the most powerful gift we have. In a similar vein, Jesus shows Eadie during her experience that our actions have what is called a "ripple effect."[42] When we act with fear and hurt others, or wrong them, the recipient of that act commits a similar act and thus creates a chain reaction. Why are these two situations important? First, it teaches us that we are here to learn unconditional love and how to treat one another with kindness. Second, we are here to learn that our actions, whether kind or cruel, have a ripple effect, since all souls are spiritually connected.

As I stated earlier, most NDEs generally experience traveling through a dark tunnel until they reach the other side. While most address their expedition into the white light after traversing the dark tunnel, some purport having experienced a "gray space" prior to their ascent into the other world. In *Secrets of the Light*, Dannion Brinkley describes his journey into what he terms the "blue-gray place."[43] In his previous NDE, Brinkley quickly traversed this space; however, upon his second sojourn, he was "forced" to reside there for observation. Brinkley learns that this space was comprised of souls consumed in their feelings of depression and thoughts of fear, dejection, and mental anguish. These souls, being from all walks of life, were unable to accept the actual ending of their lives, desired to rectify unfinished business, or were consumed by resentment and anger.[44] It is unclear about the purpose of this space and whether it exists for one to learn how to forgive themselves and others.

Ritchie presents a similar but more frighteningly intense narration of his experience into what he calls the wide, flat plain, or realm of disembodied spirits.[45] In this dwelling space, Ritchie witnessed spirits engaged in endless fighting, punching, biting, kicking, and gouging. These spirits, he notes, were consumed in their hatred, lust, despair, and negative patterns of thought.[46] Both Brinkley and Ritchie point out that those souls resided in that dark space out of choice, emphasizing that they were never abandoned. Further, in Ritchie's account, he speaks of angels hovering over this dark realm, attending to these souls in attempts to help them.[47] The law of free will exists all throughout the universe, even in this dark space where souls can reject or accept help.

I have not had a near-death experience and cannot say I have consciously left my body to traverse the realms of the unknown. I have, however, been shown by the angels that during the point of progressing into the "netherworlds," people may cross a bridge, walk through gates, or glide through a billowy black tunnel. On a personal note, my grandfather had the great fortune of dying for ten minutes. While being pronounced dead, he was actually immersed in a deep conversation with what he called *beings of light*. According to him, upon his death, he traveled out of his body only to witness the doctors calling his death below. Appearing before him were three figures of light, who were shapeless and faceless. My grandfather's first thought: "Shit, I haven't been to church in years!" Of course this was his first thought. These beings then proceeded to tell him that life wasn't about attending church, and gently reiterated to him not to worry or fear. Communicating to him by their minds alone, these forces of light showed him the importance of listening to his spirit. My grandfather saw frames of his life where he had listened and where it served him well. He was then shown when he ignored it and where it led him. They relayed to him a message about life being eternal, but as it stood, he had unfinished business here on Earth, so he wouldn't be leaving anytime soon. My grandfather returned to his body and, upon recovery, told my father of his experience, who then relayed it to me. My grandfather passed away six years later.

Earthbound Spirits

I have been told by the angels that during transition, we have the option to stay on Earth to attend our funeral and reassure our loved ones of our continued existence and safety. However, this window in Earth time lasts for about seven to ten days. After this, the portal of light that guides us to cross over begins to dim, and then the window closes. Some souls choose to leave, but others, for fear of what awaits them on the other side, or because of their strong attachments to the Earth, and to their anger, or even addictions, choose to stay in their disembodied state among the people of the Earth. These spirits are commonly referenced in New Age circles as "Earthbound spirits."

In his NDE, Ritchie witnesses Earthbound spirits in action. In particular, Ritchie relays the story of a drunken sailor at a bar on a naval base.[48] Surprisingly, he is shown that some of these men were actually not men at all, but Earthbound spirits trying to pick up glasses of whiskey to satisfy their addiction, but were unable to do so. Ritchie is further shown that in our natural state, while incarnated here on Earth, we possess a natural shield of protection engulfing our bodies, which he calls a "cocoon of light."[49] In one particular incident, Ritchie bears witness to a weakened shield as one of the living sailors became intoxicated. Once his defenses were "down," due to his intoxification, Ritchie witnesses one of the disembodied souls quickly jump into the cracked shield of the drunken sailor and altogether disappear.[50] Ritchie was then shown this scene again through different sailors. He concluded that these Earthbound spirits maintained strong Earthly attachments to their addiction and thus opted to remain in this realm rather than transition to the light. The law of free will is universal and applies to disembodied spirits as well.

Eadie also references similar experiences in her account. She claims that individuals who have deep attachments to the world, whether those are of greed, or appetites of the body, have a very difficult time transitioning home and thus become bound to the Earth.[51] Eadie further adds that once these spirits learn to sever these attachments and accept help from a greater source of power, they are able to progress toward the light.[52] Learning about Earthbound spirits can be frightening, but rest assured that angels and other light beings are always ready, available, and more than willing to help rescue these souls and lead them to the light.

In *Testimony of Light*, Frances Banks, a deceased nun channeled by the nun Helen Greaves, provides a channeled message that sheds light on rescue missions undertaken by very strong spirits and light beings.[53] In her message, she details the efforts made by these light workers, who descend into what she terms the "lower levels," in an attempt to rescue spirits choosing to stay in an unpeaceful state of being.[54] According to Banks, these missions are always underway. She emphasizes, however, that spirits are never forced to leave; they leave by their own free will. The job of the light worker is to encourage the spirit and to spread love and light to help the spirit understand and accept their past-life choices and decisions and accept the unconditional forgiveness that is available to them.

Welcoming Party

During her NDE, Eadie attends a "greeting party" filled with angelic beings, her guides, and friends.[55] She describes this as a graduation party. During this party, she is told that this party, or greeting of sorts, occurs after this transition. In *Life after Life*, one documented NDE patient explains that upon death, she encountered the most welcoming committee.[56] She notes being in the company of those she knew in past lives, as well as her grandmother and many other spirits.

Past-life and life-between-life hypnotherapy sessions from Michael Newton's work *Journey of Souls* have produced narratives that bear an impressive resemblance to NDEs.[57] These sessions reveal the commonplace experience of being received by a reception committee, or greeting party, after death.[58] This greeting party consists of guides, departed loved ones, and those from previous lives. After the greeting party, spirits are taken to places of healing and then meet individually with their spirit guide for a private conference.

Healing

Upon reviewing channeled works and hypnotherapy accounts, it appears that souls experience a variety of healing modalities directly after the transition from our Earthly experience. In *Testimony*, Banks speaks of going straight to a healing facility of sorts directly upon death.[59] Additionally, she references waking up in a rest home, where souls are placed for healing prior to their departure further into the light. In this temporary rest home, she is presided over by a group of caretakers who appear to be nurses and doctors. While there, Banks learns to adjust to the transition and help acclimate new arrivals. As in many other accounts, she, too, reports the necessity of the life review. However, she notes that neither she nor other spirits is forced to review their life immediately upon arrival. They are allotted as much time as they wish to have.

Unlike many NDEs, Bank's account of the life review is unique and provides an incomparable window into the extraordinary process. Within her consciousness, she notes, exists two blueprints reflecting details of her initial plan: the first, as she descended into matter, or Earth, and the second, as she manifested results as she experienced it.[60] Given the degree of intensity of one's experience on Earth, the actual comparative review can be harsh and overwhelming, thus leaving some of the spirits stuck until they are able to digest their actions, decisions, and missed opportunities.[61] The most important element in her account addresses this idea of judgment by God. Similar to in many NDEs, Banks declares that during this intense life review process, you, not God, nor anyone or anything else, are the judge and the jury.[62] She also points out that spirits in this phase of review are not abandoned to lament their life but instead are provided guides or helpers to assist their understanding and acceptance. This peaceful resting place is created at this stage for spirits prior to their departure to another level of understanding and growth.

In *Journey*, clients also describe undergoing a shower of healing to rehabilitate returning souls.[63] In one case, the client describes bathing in a shower of light that helps souls "purge the negativity" and harsh impact on their soul from their recent life.[64] From there, they work with their guide to review their life. After completing the hard work of the life review, souls then migrate to other levels of learning until they are ready, yet again, to incarnate either on Earth or another world compatible for learning.

Why is all of this important? My goal is to supply an alternate perception about Hell and the afterlife to assist you in stripping away layers of fear while pursuing this path. The pervading portraiture of Hell involves a hot pit of pain, sorrow, and eternal punishment engulfed in flames for those not listed in the holy book of life. In the Bible, it appears that there are only two places composing the afterlife: Heaven and Hell. But remember, Jesus tells us that in the afterlife, his father has many mansions. Narrated NDE accounts support Jesus's claim and identify the existence of multiple levels in the afterlife. If there are many places for souls to go, then how is that decided? It is necessary to visit the law of attraction here. In this law, it is stated that all conscious beings are simply energy embodying a particular vibration. According to this law, like is attracted to like, and therefore all beings are naturally attracted to other beings with the same vibration.

This law pertains to the afterlife as well. Each level embodies a specific vibration ranging from high to low or light to dense. On the basis of your rate of vibration after death, your soul will naturally gravitate to the level whose vibration corresponds to your own. Therefore, you gravitate to a place composed of a group of souls similar to your own energy level. It was also revealed to me that God does not send your soul to a particular level after his judgment of your soul. There is no judgment as we have come to understand it with an accusatory and unforgiving god. God is unconditionally loving and unconditionally forgiving, and his laws are immutable. Rather, souls inherently know of which level they belong. Most souls feel an intense discomfort if they travel to, and occupy, levels that do not correspond to their own vibration, and that you can call "Hell." I cannot personally speak about what exists within these realms. I have read that some levels correspond to the depth of one's spiritual development, which also may be so. As spirits first and foremost, we are constantly evolving and expanding. It is my hope that my presentation of the afterlife will help dismantle your fears about spending eternity in Satan's lair because you sought beyond the church for understanding and trusted God to reveal himself unto you directly.

Second, it is vital to remember that there is no death and that life is eternal. This is the message of the "resurrection"—the demonstration that there is no death and that within this physical suit of armor lies our spirit, or our eternal life force. For some, the resurrection of Jesus is literal in that his actual physical body rose, but I have been shown differently. The spirit that inhabited the body of Jesus the Christ rose, as all our spirits do, to return home. In my own personal vision, I was shown that Jesus's body was dead, but his spirit ascended—with the spirit being the emphasis. In this vision, Jesus's spirit was cloaked in illumined gold as he ascended toward the sun. Jesus did not "defeat death" as I have been told by my guide, but demonstrated that there is no death, only a spiritual release from the host body. God does not need the body, since it has already served its function. This point is made in I Corinthians, where it is noted that "*flesh and blood cannot enter the kingdom of God.*"[65] Our souls are in a constant state of evolution and death, since we know that it is only an evolutionary or transitory state. Death is not finality, and given the information provided here by various accounts, we can see that it simply lifts the veil of forgetfulness that has the unfortunate effect of temporarily deafening and blinding our consciousness. There is no Devil with a pitchfork waiting for you to torture you or claim your soul because of the "sins" committed while on Earth. Death is not a punishment, and all souls enter the kingdom of Heaven. Rather, we are our own judge, which requires unabashed accountability and truth.

What is real, however, is the potency of our negative thoughts and actions. As spirits, we have free will and thus are allowed to create at the base level, or darkest depths of our soul. These we do of our own free will. Some of these actions are harmful or unacceptable in some cultures and are, therefore, deemed "sinful." I have been shown by the Archangel Michael that what we define as sins are simply mistakes enacted by the fear, ignorance, and defensiveness of our egos. In a sense, you could say that we are tormenting our own souls by our negative thought forms or negative consciousness. The Devil, as we understand him, is not waiting to capture our souls if you reclaim the gifts of spirit given to you by God.

Lastly, it is crucial to briefly address the whole business of Jesus returning to awaken the dead during the second coming. Many Christians are waiting for the return of the Messiah to awaken and reclaim the righteous and generate a new Earth. But we have already been given the tools and knowledge to awaken ourselves through Jesus's spiritual teachings and his demonstrations. What are we waiting for? If we eagerly seek the gifts of spirit; utilize them to heal, bless, and rehabilitate the world; and love as he did unconditionally, then through us a new Earth shall be created. As stated by St. Teresa of Avila, "Christ has no body but yours; no hands, no feet on Earth but yours. Yours are the eyes through which his compassion looks out upon the world. Yours are the feet with which he walks to do good. Yours are the hands with which he blesses all the world."[66]

CHAPTER 6

Lessons from Beyond the Veil

As I channeled the life purposes and past lives of my family and my sister's friends, I learned these things:

1. We truly do have a particular purpose or mission. We all have unique talents and gifts. Some of us are painters, singers, speakers, teachers, dancers, and healers. By fulfilling this mission and by doing what we love, we shine and extend our light into the world and heal other people of the Earth. Everyone planned their mission and life lessons before arriving onto this Earth plane. However, the difficulty lies in *remembering* this mission. Further, upon incarnation onto this plane, we enter a veil of forgetfulness, and what we think we know for sure is that we are our bodies, and that we have only five senses, and that Earth is the only reality. We believe we are limited to the thinking of this world and are indoctrinated as such. We are taught from childhood that we truly belong to *this* world.

As we grow up, we watch our parents subscribe to the "ways" of this world and serve as witnesses to their successes and failures, as deemed by this world. As people, we aspire to find great, profitable jobs that will reflect the image we hope to craft and externally convey. Somehow, along the way through our evolution from adolescent to adult, we shut off our dreams and our heart's desires to learn how to be of this world and succeed in this world. Although we have bought in to the grand narrative of success, status, and legitimacy of the material world, our heart will attempt to guide us to create for ourselves, through a vision of love, the life we want. This is usually in accord with the dreams of our childhood and in true alignment with our life purpose or mission. These dreams come from the innocence and love we embody as children, and it is through the pursuit of these dreams with love, kindness, compassion, and desire that we complete our mission. People today speak of dreams as pure impossibility, fantasies, and unrealized hopes. We have forgotten our true selves as divine beings who know of no limitations and cannot truly conceptualize, at our core, impossibility.

2. Everyone must balance their karmic debt: The universe is organized according to very specific objective laws. One of those laws is the law of balance or karma. This law states that there must be equilibrium in all things, and therefore all action and energy must be stabilized and balanced. All our actions dispatch energy throughout the universe and must be reciprocated in like and kind. Some of this circulated energy may be light and weightless, and some is incredibly dense. According to this law, in order for there to be equilibrium, we must receive that which we give, whether in this lifetime or in the next. There is no punishment operating within the universe, since the creator is only love. As cocreators and divine beings we operate according to these laws. Upon investigating previous lives, I learned of my countless errors and mistakes and was shown my contributions of love as well. In this lifetime, I am repaying those debts or balancing the scales of my being, as many of us are.

3. Everyone has life lessons: All of us are here to learn many lessons that we selected before our actual physical incarnation. Some of us have a laundry list, while for others, the list may be shorter. Through many channeling sessions, I became aware of the variety of life lessons one could experience. The angels told me the lessons I chose, which included forgiveness and self-love, joy, patience, surrender, and even happiness. For some, there are lessons of humility, acceptance, and trust. However, for almost all, the lessons of love and forgiveness are two of the biggest lessons. These lessons manifest in the form of life's challenges. People may battle a lifelong illness or struggle with physical ailments, abandonment, betrayal, and abuse, in order to fully learn the lesson selected prior to their actual physical birth. These lessons enable us to grow spiritually and move us into a state of wholeness as we learn to embody all attributes of our divine self.

4. We choose our family: We choose our parents and siblings, and we choose them to balance our karma with them from previous lifetimes and to learn lessons with them for spiritual growth. However, the most important reason is that these beautiful spirits are some of our greatest lifelong teachers. They teach us profound lessons of unconditional love, acceptance, and forgiveness. And while it is true that we have created karma with some of them from previous lives that must be balanced, it is also important that we realize that these spirits want you to succeed. For some, this is certainly difficult to believe, because at times we have been punished by our parents and family members and have suffered great ills because of them. In most instances, we may not have had the control to change the circumstances of our upbringing, or the actions of our parents, sisters, or brothers, but we do have control over how we respond to them. Most of our deepest lessons are learned when we open our hearts and respond to the call for forgiveness and love. This is, of course, easier said than done.

Divine Laws of the Universe

As I studied and channeled information from the angelic realms, I further learned about objective laws that structure and support our universe. I found these to be useful and helpful when attempting to understand our psychic identity and its relationship to the function of the universe. Understanding these laws is important for development of the psychic self, since they reveal how the universe operates and how your life exists in relation to them. These laws include the Law of Balance, Law of Attraction, Law of One, and the Law of Love. Knowledge of these laws helps us dismantle negative thought patterns. Prior to my awareness of these laws, I was invested in the laws of guilt, fear, victimhood, and sin. Specifically, the belief that the universe is against us and our own personal development. These laws stand in stark contrast to the metaphysical principle that God's universe operates and sustains itself on the energy of love. Moreover, in the realm of Christianity is the idea of separation between God and man, as if our identity is its own. However, as noted in spiritual law, an identity separate from God is impossible. It is obviously comforting to know that we are truly made in the image of God, which includes pure divine love and its attributes. Additionally, this means that our communion with God is eternal, since we are permanently joined.

Understanding these laws is truly a part of the psychic journey, since it involves understanding our identity, our source, our pure potential, and our power. Please note that there are many universal laws; however, I am including the most-pertinent laws conducive to the messages being presented in this book.

LAW OF BALANCE OR KARMA

This law states that the energy of every action in the universe must be reproduced in like and kind. The universe is harmonious, and while we are here on Earth our actions must be balanced within this particular dimension. This law is intimately intertwined with the concept of karma. Karma, as I understand it, is simply the law of cause and effect, meaning that we create a cause and at some point in time shall receive its corresponding effect. The law of balance guarantees that we shall reap exactly what we sow, but never as a form of punishment. If your actions are loving, helpful, and harmless, or an embodiment of light energy, then you shall receive and experience the effects of that particular type of energy. However, if you expel a denser or darker energy in the form of deception, guilt, pain, or harm, then you will, at some point in time, be on the receiving end of the same type of lower energy. All actions must be balanced, because the universe is naturally just. As you develop your gifts, you will receive as much as you put in, and your efforts will be rewarded. Intentionality is the key. If you focus on growing your gifts solely for financial gain, without the intent to truly serve, then your gifts will expand only so far on the basis of your intentions.

THE LAW OF ATTRACTION

The knowledge of this law is already quite widespread due to the successful release of *The Secret*.[1] Simply put, this law affirms that we create our own reality by our thoughts. This law gives prominence to the mind and efficacy of our thoughts. In essence, the reality we are physically experiencing is created by the epicenter that is our mind. While many believe that our understanding derives from our experiences, it is actually our belief system that frames our experience. This law emphasizes that our thoughts, being negative or positive, create our experience. So if we wish to attract a positive experience, then we must think positively.

This law also supports common expressions such as "birds of a feather flock together," "like attracts like," and "show me your friends and I'll tell you who you are." In our lives, we attract unto ourselves people who are similar in thought. They essentially mirror our own personal beliefs and current judgments. It is essential to understand why you must have at least a basic understanding of this law. Throughout your development as a psychic, you will attract a multitude of experiences based upon your consciousness at the time. Knowing that your thoughts create your reality will help you manage the magnitude of your growth as a psychic. What I mean by this is that as long as you can manage your mind, and thoughts, and align them with your higher self, you will have expanded your capacity for psychic growth and understanding, and the universe will bring you these experiences that allow for your growth as a psychic.

THE LAW OF ONE

This law simply states that all consciousness exists in the divine mind that is God. It further articulates that everything is mental and that all minds are joined in the mind of God. This particular law can also be called the law of interconnection. All things in the universe and here on our tiny planet, including people, are divinely interwoven and connected. Therefore, all thoughts are joined and our actions and thoughts have an effect on one another mentally, emotionally, and physically. It is useful here to use the analogy of the pebble and the ocean. If you throw a pebble into the ocean of life, it creates a ripple effect throughout the body of water, thus affecting the whole in some way. When we as individuals reach for loving thoughts and act from love, it creates a ripple effect of loving energy throughout the human race.

THE LAW OF LOVE

Love governs all of creation and structures all universal spiritual laws. God is love, and thus the offspring, or the children of God, are unquestionably pure love. Love is the purest form of creative power and transformation in the universe. The psychic ministry is structured by the law of love and is of itself a service of love. The gifts that are given derive from our creator with the purpose of healing people through love. Psychics can access a consciousness of love, which is not of themselves, that can help facilitate healing of the mind and the heart.

CHAPTER 7

Endings and Beginnings

My bond with Orion strengthened the more I channeled him. We discussed out-of-body travel at night and spiritual divination tools such as the Tarot. While I was happy with the level of communication between myself and my guide, I was eager to move on to trance channeling and asked Orion when we could begin. Trance channeling is a process whereby the body and mind of a channeler falls into a deep, trancelike state, allowing for the consciousness of another entity to inhabit their body for the purposes of communication.[1] The mannerisms then exhibited by the channeler will likely shift and reflect those of the being inhabiting the body. I felt it would be an easier method to replace the enormous amount of writing I was doing. He explained to me that it was indeed possible, but it would take time, practice, and a lot of trust. I was not deterred. Since trance channeling was not an easy transition, I just practiced repeating what I heard and recorded it into a device. This was very tricky because I interrupted my guide and angels to complete a previous sentence; this disrupted the natural flow of energy streaming through my consciousness. As I was taught, angels and guides do not speak to us using actual words as we understand them. They send us waves of energy that translate into words. When that wavelength is interrupted, because of our thoughts, doubts, and fears, it can make maintaining the connection difficult.

I repeatedly asked Orion to transition into trance channeling and thought I was ready to relinquish control of my body. Unfortunately, there was no hint of shifting into that mode of communication. It has been very challenging to accept that there is a divine order and timing for all things. Impatiently, I wanted everything to progress on my own time according to my terms. This, of course, is not how the universe operates. As spirits operating within this dense terrain, we have a limited perception of what is best for us and our growth. But truly, the universe objectively knows the overall best methods for our growth, and the appropriate time for us to blossom and expand.

After months of channeling Orion, I felt I had always known him. In one session, he expressed our relationship as ball and chain throughout many lifetimes. I viewed him as my elder brother, my friend, and my confidant. He saw me at my worst and my best, and there were no secrets in my life that he did not have knowledge of. I relied on Orion always being there any time I reached for him. As he stated, "I am here for you to call on, during great pleasures, times of pain, and through doubt, which you do express, but overcome like the mighty oak, you stand tall as well."

It was during the third week of September that I again asked Orion to practice trance channeling. I never gave up on anything easily. I began the day like all the others, with prayer, meditation, and running. I sat down on my bed near the bay window, held my black tape recorder in my hand, and closed my eyes. I prayed and invited the angels and Orion to converse with me that morning. There was a short pause before I felt a wave of energy move toward me. At the beginning of this channeling session, I spoke with the angels about my life purpose and my personal goals. Toward the end of this conversation, Orion came forward and explained in depth about my future role on this planet. While I was asking Orion for more clarification, he abruptly interrupted me and insisted, "We must end our conversation for the lord thy God has willed it." This sharp interruption was very unexpected. Why did God not want us to speak? I was worried and incredibly nervous. I wondered if I had abused my power. Was I not supposed to be channeling like this? I panicked and paced back and forth in my bedroom. What had I done? I attempted to channel again one hour afterward, but things were not clear.

I asked the angels for answers about my guide for several days without success. Where was my guide? He had conveyed to me before that he would be with me until I crossed back over to the other side. I learned that when you're in a state of panic and anxiety, it is much harder to channel, and the messages you *do* receive are likely from your ego.

It took at least five days for me to receive a message about the situation at hand. I asked the archangels to explain why my spirit guide was no longer available. As per the archangels:

Well, dear one, he has gone to learn lessons, for he is here to help you on your path toward God dear one. We say he will return shortly. He has gone off to learn lessons that will help you both on this side—the Earth plane, dear one, lessons from which you will benefit. For God is with you.

I haven't heard from Orion since that day. I attempted to reach him countless times, but to no avail. I knew that guides intermittently moved in and out of your life depending on your current life lesson, but I was under the impression that Orion was my guide until I transitioned home. Unable to reach Orion, I dedicated my channeling sessions to communing with the angels for messages.

In October my boyfriend and I moved from San Francisco to Oakland. He received a great job, and it was cheaper for us to live in that city. Initially, I was anxious. We were moving for the third time since we had moved to California, and I still barely knew my way around. I asked the angels the reason for the move. They explained that there were many people to help in Oakland, as there were in every part of the world. We settled into a small, two-bedroom apartment, and I finished my dissertation. In my heart, I celebrated the completion of this cycle of my life. Although I was grateful for the lessons I learned during these seven arduous years, I was ready to venture into the next chapter of my life.

Unexpectedly during my first month in Oakland, I met a new guide during a simple meditation. I was focused on making myself a clear and balanced channel and heard a voice in the room. The voice was not loud, but it was breathy, much like all the other voices I've heard with my outer ears throughout the years. The voice revealed a name, which I heard with my left ear. It whispered, "Josiah." I opened my eyes and looked around the room to see if anyone was there. The room was empty, so I continued with my meditation. Afterward, I sat down at my kitchen table and asked the angels for clarification about Josiah.

During a few of my previous experiences in meditation, some spirits stepped forward to meet me without announcing their presence or their name. Although a majority of them had been helpful, I wanted to confirm the nature of this being's intentions toward me. I focused my energy toward the archangels and asked for clarity about this light being. Truthfully, I was nervous. My heart was hoping for a guide to lead me or help me further develop my skills. The archangels revealed to me that he was a good light being available to help me. Before I could think of my next question, Josiah came forward and introduced himself:

> *Why child, it is I, Josiah, lord of light, descended down upon thee this day forth, to be a witness. Why, I say, it was truly an honor to watch thee this day forward, to see all the works of the lord thy god. Why, you ask, why have I come down upon thee this day forth? I came at God's command to watch thee, help thee, lift thee up to the light of God. I have come down upon thee to help thee this day forward.*

Josiah's introduction was brief. At the time, I believed I had just met my new guide, Josiah. Although I was excited to know that I had new help, I was also sad and mourned the loss of Orion. Unfortunately, I misunderstood Josiah's role. I thought he was a replacement guide for Orion, but I was wrong. It took over one year to learn that he was among a collective of elemental guides to teach me how to manifest my dreams.

I attempted to channel Josiah casually throughout the month of October. I could feel his energy among many others, but I could never see him. I tried multiple times a day but was unsuccessful. There were moments where I attempted to speak with Josiah, but the archangels interceded to answer all my questions. I found communication with Josiah increasingly difficult the more I tried. I was unable to determine why this was happening and why I could not see him. My frustration grew, and quite frankly I felt inadequate. I knew I wasn't alone, but I felt sadness about the situation. I believed I had taken several steps back and had to start from the ground up with someone new.

I was satisfied with my psychic practice, but I was ready to take classes and prayed to find one in the area. I wasn't sure what type of class I wanted to take, and to be truthful, I did not know the true limitations or the extent of my abilities either. I had chosen channeling and Tarot as my gifts, but I needed a community and more practice. Did I want to take a course strictly devoted to Tarot? Did I want to take a course on mediumship and learn to connect to deceased loved ones? Did I want to learn about healing to heal the sick by divine light, or did I want to be an actual psychic reader? The psychic world can be very overwhelming, and I decided to experiment more at the beginning of my development.

After a couple of weeks settling into our new neighborhood, I searched online for a class. A little book store by the name of Healing Light popped up onto the screen. Many metaphysical classes were held there every month, and to top it off, the store was located only three miles from my house. The website stated that a mediumship class was held in the store, and I decided to go and check it out for myself.

I pulled up to a two-story pink building on the corner of MLK in Berkeley. The door bells chimed as I walked through the entrance. The front room smelled of lavender, sage, and citrus notes, and statues of angels, gnomes, and fairies populated the glass shelves. I walked back to the main room and browsed many books, candles, oracle cards, and buddha figurines. The owner of the store approached me as I was browsing the containers of crystals. She introduced herself and asked if this was my first time in the store. I told her I was new to the area and inquired about mediumship classes. I am not sure why I asked for that class in particular, but it rolled off my tongue. The owner relayed to me that she did not know when the classes would begin again and that she needed at least four people to take the class for it to make; I gave her my number to call me once she found three other people. I was incredibly hopeful, but not certain when I would ever be able to take my first actual class.

Two weeks passed and I received a phone call from the owner. She informed me that three other people inquired about the mediumship class, and she asked if I was still interested. I replied that I would love to take the class, and I signed up for the course. The introductory mediumship course was four weeks long and ended one week before my dissertation defense. The class took place on Friday nights for two hours. I was anxious and very excited to be with like-minded people.

A few weeks later, I pulled up to the store and prayed in my car before entering the classroom. A short Filipino woman with black glasses and long, black hair walked into the room and introduced herself as the instructor. Slowly, three other females walked into the room and sat down. The class was structured unconventionally; there were no handouts or direct instructions. In this class, we sat in a circle in a dark room lit by tea candles. The instructor told us to ground and protect ourselves and close our eyes to meditate. The teacher asked us to begin identifying spirits in the room. Immediately she was pulling the names of deceased spirits who were joining us. Two of the students also felt spirits in the room, but I did not. My teacher continued to describe the spirits as she felt them. In my mind's eye, I would see only flashes of pictures, but nothing definitive. Truthfully, I felt out of my league. It must have been at least one hour that we meditated in this room, when I felt my mind extend further across the veil.

Awakening the Psychic Self

Unexpectedly, I found myself staring into a dark layer of outer space. A large, golden disc emerged in this black, quiet space, which appeared to be lying flat on a black surface. Within a few moments, the center of the disk opened up and a little gnome popped through and climbed out. He placed the lid back into the disk and thoroughly examined me behind his wire-rimmed glasses. I decided to avoid questioning what I was seeing. I learned that if I interrupted my connection with other realms, the connection would break, because the logic and reasoning side of my brain would doubt or question the reality of what was being shown.

The gnome gestured with his hand for me to follow him to a set of curtains. The gnome, wearing little, round spectacles and a small, red cap, placed his finger over his mouth, commanding my silence before he parted the veil. I nodded in compliance and he slowly separated the curtain. I focused my attention behind the veil and witnessed a colorful scene full of waterfalls and glistening rocks. Dolphins jumped in and out of the water, and mermaids swam under the creamy blue waterfalls. My eyes grew bigger in disbelief as the scene unfolded. It looked like a scene animated by Walt Disney himself! The colors were extremely vivid and surreal. The gnome closed the curtains and took me to another veil. Again, he gestured by putting his finger to his mouth, and I nodded in agreement. His little fingers parted the curtains. Before me was a large fire pit in the center of the woods, with people and other creatures, such as a Minotaur, dancing around it performing some sort of fire ritual or ceremony. The curtains closed and the gnome looked at me, trying to gauge whether or not I understood what I was being shown. I smiled, nodded, and prepared myself for the next scene.

The instructor interrupted the class before I could shift to the next scene. She asked if anyone else had felt gnome energy in the room. Instantly, I was thrilled. I actually *did* see a gnome, but he was gone. We continued to meditate for almost another hour and shared what we were seeing throughout our circle. At the very end of the class, my teacher asked if anyone knew a woman named *Wynona*. Stunned, I said, "Yes. That's my step-grandmother." She continued to ask me if my grandmother knew anyone by the name of Sally. I truly did not know but figured I would ask my mother. I felt comfortable in the class and enjoyed being with the students. However, I hoped that my instructor would provide detailed instructions in the coming weeks.

In the following two classes, we practiced tuning in to each other's spirit guides and bringing in the spirits of deceased loved ones. I expected that the teacher would provide specific directions, but unfortunately she did not. We sat next to our partners and attempted to figure out how to tune in to one another's spirit guide. To my surprise, I was able to see my partner's guide and provide a detailed message.

During the third week in class, each student brought in a photo of a deceased loved one. As we sat in a circle with a little lit tea light, the teacher directed us to tune in to the loved one in the photo. Again, we attempted to do this without actual direction. We passed our pictures around the room to each student and closed our eyes. Our teacher asked us to tune in to receive a message. I was indeed able to hear the voices of those we sought to speak with during class. But I was slightly disappointed due to the lack of direction.

The last class was bittersweet. I was sad to end the course, primarily because I would no longer have a community in which to practice with, but I was also proud of the work I'd done over the past four weeks. At the end of the course, my teacher gave us our certificates and we all parted ways. She informed us about the intermediate course, and we all agreed to attend. The following week I returned to Austin, Texas, to defend my dissertation.

I returned to the university to study and make changes to a few of my chapters. I visited an old friend whom I knew I probably would not see again. I additionally visited the old laboratory where I used to work. I walked around and thought about the many endless nights I worked on papers, grants, and scholarships, and even though at that time I may not have known or acknowledged it, I knew that the angels and my guides helped me through that process. I went through each cabinet to see if I had left anything behind, but there was nothing I wished to take. I said my goodbyes and walked out of that space for the last time.

Upon my return home, my mother and father shared their own current spiritual experiences. One evening my mother told me that our neighbor, whom I knew growing up, wanted to speak with me. She was going through her own spiritual questioning and wanted some clarity or assistance. I was truly nervous to disclose my own experiences, and I was afraid of being crucified regarding my own beliefs, which were still being crafted on a daily basis. I decided to meet with her anyway and prayed that divine healing and messages would lovingly flow through me.

A few nights later I walked two houses down and knocked on my neighbor's door. She was very happy to see me. I sat in the kitchen as she was preparing a huge meal for a family reunion. She explained her personal struggles with questioning her beliefs and her perception of God while blending and mixing her secret macaroni-and-cheese mixture. After all, she too was raised in a very structured Christian household. Her family was concerned about her new spiritual ideas about why we are here, who we are, and what God truly is.

According to them, she was committing a major sin, and the very thought of her shifting her perception about God was a violation of God's written truth. From the truth of my heart, I shared with her what I knew to be true for me, which was that God, as I knew him, was pure love. And that was my truth and personal definition. I no longer chose to believe in a God of condemnation, fear, sin, or even judgment. Through prayer, meditation, and much study, I knew for myself that these beliefs were mere choices, and as such, we become reflections of the God we serve.

During that time, we discussed my experiences, and I shared what knowledge I had acquired from the angelic realm. Before I left she asked me to look into her life purpose and past lives. Although she was moving toward retirement, she was still searching for what it was that she came here to do. And for me, it was my joy to lend a helping hand any way I could. I returned home and prayed for guidance and a clear indication of her mission.

I returned a few days later with messages from the angels. I presented her with stories of her past incarnations on this Earth plane, which truly resonated with her. I also shared with her information about her mission, which deep within she already knew. I've learned that many of the people I channeled for already knew their purpose or their mission here. I have come to find that most are just afraid to take a risk to follow their heart and their dreams.

The morning of my defense I was incredibly nervous. I prayed all morning as I got dressed. I opened my laptop to double-check that I sent my presentation to my advisor for review. When I lifted my laptop I saw the time: 4:44. I instantly knew that the angels were with me. My mother, who was notorious for being late, was also late driving me to my defense. I arrived, somehow, on time.

I was nervous throughout my entire defense. But it was actually easier than I had expected—almost seemingly beyond easy—and I knew that this was the handiwork of God. I passed with edits. I made those edits within four days and submitted my dissertation. I was finished. Completely. That chapter of my life was over. I couldn't wait to return home and begin a new cycle in my life.

CHAPTER 8

Psychic Hurdles

I returned to Oakland completely ready to begin my new life. Truthfully, I had no idea what type of job I would apply for or what I was going to do. I had a little bit of money to live on for four months, which I felt was more than enough to keep as a safety net until I found a suitable position. January and February were spent applying for academic positions that paid well. I wrote countless cover letters and created various styles of resumes during the day and read books and channeled messages in the evening.

I felt as if I had two full-time jobs. Initially, I wasn't worried about landing a great job. After all, I just finished obtaining my PhD and had great skills and a well-composed resume. I was conservative with my money and kept plugging away at job applications. My boyfriend and I celebrated New Year's Eve at his friend's house, but I was eager to go home and meditate to communicate with my guides about the upcoming year.

On New Year's morning I woke up early to meditate and pray. I sat on the little white love seat in my living room and prepared to communicate with my guide after grounding and protecting myself. I asked my guide and angels to show me what was in store for the year. I did not expect to see much, but I was hopeful. After ten minutes I could feel myself slipping deeper into my meditation. I saw one of my guides, White Cloud, sitting on a throne. He grabbed my hand to help me climb a small set of stairs leading to an undecorated throne beside him. He asked me, "You want to know what's in store for you this year?" I nodded my head. He picked up a wand and said, "Let's ask grandmother moon what she sees." The windows flew open and a small vortex of light circled around the moon.

The first image that appeared was that of a middle-aged Chinese man walking toward me, holding two large scales. He stopped in front of me and showed me that the scales were balanced. I acknowledged my understanding of the symbol, and the image faded. I was then shown another scene. I saw myself in a room with another person reading the Tarot. My guides followed this image with that of a flying butterfly, which then shifted to a grasshopper. The butterfly and the grasshopper moved along together and then shifted to an elephant, which then reverted back into a butterfly.

Last, I was shown a double-handed ceramic vessel placed under a faucet. The water dripped incredibly slowly into the vessel, and I felt myself become impatient and annoyed as the water dripped from the faucet. Suddenly, the scene shifted and the vessel was placed outdoors and a storm rolled in. Rainwater filled the vessel quickly and the water began to overflow. A large, white lightning bolt from the sky struck the vessel, and it shattered into pieces. This was the last image that appeared to me. I asked for clarification, but none was given. While some of the symbols were not necessarily clear, I understood that this year would be about transformation and learning to balance different aspects of my life.

Over the next two months I noticed a change with my spiritual vision. My inner eye appeared clogged. The images within my purview were being shown through a filter of sorts; the pictures were a bit scrambled and colorless. I tried, to no avail, to make the images clearer. I noticed that my clairaudience, too, was suffering. Channeling had become increasingly difficult, and I was no longer able to hear the voices of the angels or my guide. Initially I wasn't too worried about the problems I was experiencing with my sight and my clairaudience. I thought somehow they would miraculously return.

I decided to further my mediumship practice and signed up for an intermediate mediumship class, which began in February. My teacher informed me one week prior that not all the students from my introductory course could afford to take the course for at least another month, and she encouraged me to take this course with a new group. I agreed and showed up for the class on Friday nights, which consisted of four women and one male who was blind.

The first week of class I struggled. I could not see, hear, or even feel. The second week was the same. The third week we went to visit the house of a woman who claimed it was haunted. I prayed for major assistance from my guide, and it was given. I asked for help so that I could see, or at least hear *something*. The house was a small, rickety box that was probably built some time in the 1950s. Upon meeting the owner, it was clear that she struggled with drug addiction.

The house encompassed an uncomfortable energy. I felt in my bones a sense of sickness, uneasiness, and even desperation. The interior of the house was dimly lit, and a row of mirrors lined the back wall of the owner's bedroom and living room. My classmates and I walked through the front room and the kitchen and then out into the backyard. Everyone in my class could feel the spirits roaming around. I felt disappointed and frustrated that I couldn't sense the spirits, and asked my guides for help. They responded, "We know you cannot see or feel much right now, but just try to listen." I took a series of deep breaths and asked who was present. And to my surprise, I heard two female names. I asked them why they were there, but there was no response. I moved back into the kitchen and leaned up against the door. I watched as everyone took notes on what they saw and felt. I just closed my eyes and prayed for assistance. Unexpectedly, I felt a hand graze the right side of my face and run through my hair.

My first inclination was to yell and accuse someone of toying with me, but I quickly saw that no one was around me. I closed my eyes a second time and saw an old car maintenance garage, but my vision was interrupted by my teacher calling all of us together to compare stories at the end of the tour. It turned out that my evening was a bit of a success after all. The plot was previously a mechanic's garage, and someone else had heard the same female names I had earlier. My teacher closed the circle by leading us through prayer and covering the house in the white light of God. As we imagined the light filling the space, I saw in my mind's eye a man in the kitchen who was wearing white orthopedic shoes. A curtain was being lifted above his feet, knees, and upper legs. I asked them to stop since I felt that the energy was very dense and uncomfortable.

At the end of this visit, our teacher took us out of the house, and we prayed once more and returned to our classroom. Truthfully, I felt so grateful for all the assistance I'd received that night. I finished this course although my sight and hearing were weak. I tried to explain to my teacher and classmates that something was happening to me, but I didn't know what. I wondered if I was being punished for something. Had I abused my gifts? Every day I woke up and prayed and meditated, but I could not see well, nor could I hear. Channeling was no longer available to me. What had I done? My heart was heavy and sad. Maybe the angels had decided against me. Maybe God decided that I was not the right person after all. For weeks I struggled; this became a major source of frustration in my life. Additionally, I was still searching for a job and was incredibly unsuccessful. Whatever little faith I had was slipping. Daily, I sank to my knees and cried and even begged God for help. I began to think that maybe I was alone after all.

It was the end of March and I was officially broke. All of my savings were gone, and I was depending on the love and generosity of my boyfriend to save me. During the last week of the month, I received a phone call for a position. I gladly interviewed and took the job. I was finally able to pay my bills for a few weeks at least. In mid-April it was decided that I wasn't a good fit for the company. I had expected this change, since I felt extremely uncomfortable working for this company, whose values were not in alignment with my own.

I felt an overwhelming sense of worry again. I told myself that something better was coming for me, and released my frustration and worry. At this time, I had been waiting to sign up for a Tarot class, which was set to begin in two weeks, but I was yet again unemployed and concerned about spending money. I waited one week before deciding to take it and signed up and hoped for the best.

One week later I unexpectedly received a phone call from a temp agency. A job interview for a healthcare startup company was on the table if I would consider it. My initial reaction was to say absolutely not. I'd never worked in that industry and was not the least bit interested. But my pockets and heart said, why not? The interview was the same day in San Francisco, and I took a leap of faith and decided to go for it. The interview was smooth and unbelievably easy. I knew then that I was supposed to be there, but why?

During the day I focused on being the best at my job, and at night I began to review the meanings of the Tarot cards before the class officially began. While looking for Tarot books, I was a bit overwhelmed by the amount of available material. The New Age field is inundated with Tarot books, practical Tarot exercises, and various Tarot decks. To tackle the definition of the cards, I made flashcards. The Tarot class lasted for six weeks.

When I walked into the small room at Healing Light, I saw one girl sitting in the corner of the table, and I said Hello. Two minutes later, a familiar face walked in. It was Carrie, a girl from my introductory mediumship class. We connected immediately. Our conversations consisted of all things spirit, communication, and channeling.

I studied Tarot every day and pulled a card for myself on a daily basis in a continual effort to memorize each card's meaning. At the end of the six weeks we had to read for each other. I admit that I was very nervous but enjoyed learning and practicing. I did not want to say goodbye to my new set of classmates and invited them over to my house to practice. Only a couple of them showed up, and we practiced reading cards for each other and even meditated together.

My clairvoyance and clairaudience were still majorly impaired. When I tuned in to focus and read the energy of my friends, all the incoming images were tinted yellow and fuzzy. It was as if they were being sifted through a bright-yellow filter. I had to share with my new friends the degree of my current limitations; however, I could not explain what was happening and why. As I sat with my classmates, Carrie and Penny, I explained my struggle to see well and lamented the loss of my hearing. I felt I could not contribute to helping them in any way. Truthfully, I was very embarrassed. In previous classes I shared with them some of my experiences, but how could they believe me when I could not demonstrate to them?

I felt as if I was being punished in some way. I asked the angels, God, my guides, practically anyone who was listening, what I had done wrong. But, of course, no one answered. I met weekly with Carrie and Penny and spent my time teaching them all that I had learned. Although I could no longer channel my guide or the angelic realm to help them, I figured I would educate them on all the methods I'd learned from above. I guided them through meditations and practiced various techniques to clarify, develop, and increase their vision and hearing. Although I knew I was helping both women improve their skills, I felt as if I was stuck in the same place for months. I questioned why the three of us had been brought together. Was I really there to teach them? Would they help me regain my sight and sound? What was our relationship with each other?

As we practiced, it became evident that Carrie's gifts were flourishing. Her clairaudience was beginning to expand, and her sight was phenomenal. Although I was pleased with Carrie's progress, I was dismayed at my continuous stalemate. I questioned why we had been brought together. Given that she was able to see and hear messages, Carrie offered to look into the nature of our relationship. As she sat back in a black, padded reclining chair, she closed her eyes to hear and see our connection. About two minutes in, she grabbed her chest and began panting, "War. We fought in war together, all three of us. Somewhere in Europe in the year 1600." She could feel the intense fear and refused to get any additional information. Weeks passed; we learned that the three of us have spent twenty-five lifetimes together, one being in war, the other spent as nuns, and an additional time in Egypt. We were brought together again to help each other heal wounds from previous lifetimes and to work together to bring light into the world.

Personally, I felt privileged to share the information and techniques I learned with Carrie and Penny. My heart warmed as I watched their progress, but truly on the inside I was devastated and embarrassed. After so much dedicated practice, my abilities were still absent. I prayed endlessly for help so that I could fix the problem. One early morning I sat on the couch and attempted to channel again. Even though I knew my abilities were suspended, I was so desperate that I tried anything and everything I knew, hoping to get different results. I closed my eyes and prayed and begged for an answer. I asked all the angels and archangels to answer me. I held my pen in my hand and felt pressure building up around my head. I knew an angel was there, but would I be able to hear them? To my complete surprise I heard the following message:

It's our pleasure to speak to you Deanna. We come to say we are pleased at your progress. We come to say it is with honor that we introduce ourselves; we are Gabriel, Winslow, Josiah, Ezekiel, Efron, and Nehemiah. It is our pleasure to say we are angels, blessed be. Let us begin. We are blessings from above to help you here move forward into the light of God. To move forward, as you say, is to, with grace, to extend yourself greatly. It is our great pleasure to lead the way.

Let it be known that it is I, lord Gabriel upon you. Thou art being moved forward, as it were, closer to the all that is, for it is with beneficence that this is so. For it is within the grace of God that you are there in the divine presence of our living God, the great one, the mighty Jehovah. For thou has asked to be an angel among us has thou not? Thou has proposed a question of the most high Deanna. For thou has willed it to move forward, we say, to the great one, the great and mighty one. Let it be known we are here to lead you. Gabriel comes to lead you forward Deanna. We know this has been a difficult time, but hear our thoughts. Alas, you know the truth as it were Deanna.

For thou art guided most greatly. We come to say for thou art being led by the holy masters, alas we come to greet you. It is a great honor to help you. Does thou know that thou are a great being? Thou art most greatly being served by divine beings Deanna. For those on high have come to greet you as it were, if thou art willing to hear, see. We will explain ourselves further. Listen closely. For we come upon you now to tell you of blessings to come Deanna. For there are many who greet you most greatly. Thou presence is known amongst us here in our lands of God, as angelic guides of light. Let it be known that thou is a true angel Deanna amongst us all, to be taken, lifted up as it were to the lands of God to experience death, life, healing, magnification of spirit, all of these and then some. Do you understand what we are saying?

Frightened by this revelation, I stopped channeling. Was I going to die? The content of this message unnerved me, and I had to leave the house to go to work. My heart felt a bit relieved that I was able to channel, but I was also incredibly fearful for my life. Was it already over? I spoke to no one about what I was told. I was becoming so confused. I didn't know what to think anymore anyway. Was I really to believe this? How could I trust what I was hearing now?

The rest of the week was the same. I worked the same job I truly disliked, and I felt a bit depressed about the state of my life. I thought about the message given to me by archangel Gabriel, and I was fearful. That week, as I laid my head to sleep at night, I noticed my guides or angels were attempting to garner my attention through a song. Music is the medium through which my guides passed messages to me, but it was usually upon waking that they did so. Songs began to saturate my mind as I closed my eyes at night. Initially I ignored them, but three days in, I noticed the same song repeating in my head. The lyrics spoke of leaving the Earth and dying. When I placed my head down to sleep, I was incredibly petrified. I was depressed, but I wasn't ready to die yet. I closed my eyes at night and saw flashes of green, yellow, and white light fill the room. My heart began racing and I panicked. I did not sleep at all that night, and every evening thereafter was rough, although nothing occurred.

The following week I invited Penny to my house to practice reading for each other. I guided her through a few meditations and completed a few psychometry exercises. That evening in particular I saw a large diamond in my mind's eye, tinted yellow, like everything else. I told Penny that I saw a spinning diamond for her. At the time, unbeknown to me, that diamond was a message for the three of us: Penny, Carrie, and myself.

We gathered at my house the following week to practice. After the first meditation, Carrie told us that she saw a spinning diamond, but it was meant for the three of us. At the time, we had no clue what that meant or why we all were seeing the same image. Later that night after everyone left, I received a text message from Carrie. She reported that she was told that the diamond symbolized eternity. She further informed me that her guide wanted us to meditate sitting in the shape of a pyramid, which represented the Holy Trinity, and focus on the diamond spinning among the three of us.

It was at this juncture where I began taking more risks concerning my beliefs and faith. I was more willing to practice rituals and unfamiliar or uncomfortable exercises that I would usually intentionally avoid. I didn't feel that the Devil was misguiding me at this point. Rather, I was more intent on learning what I hoped were the mysteries of the kingdom of God.

A week later, we met at my house to practice this pyramid exercise. Truthfully, Carrie did not know why we were even encouraged to do this exercise. However, we got into the habit of trusting her guide, since all of his messages were positive and informative. I knew that we were conjuring in some form, but I trusted our intentions. We sat on the floor in the shape of a pyramid and held hands. It dawned on me to ask her which position we were supposed to take. Who was to be at the top and who was to sit at the base? As we looked around, we acknowledged that we were already sitting in the correct position, with Carrie and Penny at the bottom and myself at the top. We grabbed each other's hands and closed our eyes. About four minutes in, I let go because I did not feel, see, or hear anything. I was utterly frustrated. Carrie asked why I released my hands. I told her nothing was occurring, but we tried again. I closed my eyes and waited. I saw nothing but darkness. I waited. Finally, after ten minutes, both women released my hands. I was very curious to see if either one of them experienced anything. I raised my eyes to both women in curiosity. Both Carrie and Penny were smiling. They were happy, perhaps even shocked at what they had just experienced, and I could feel my heart begin to break. Carrie recounted her vision to us. She saw the three of us taken to visit the realm of the angels. She stated that she saw the three of us welcomed by an angel as we entered the place of healing upon death.

As she entered this realm, the angel said, "You have arrived. You are now experiencing healing in all forms." Carrie heard trumpets playing amid white, fluffy clouds. She noticed that she and other surrounding spirits were dressed in white. She then heard a man's voice affirm, "You are now experiencing death." Her vision was muted into darkness and then shifted to images of oceans and birds flying. She then heard a man assert, "You are now experiencing life." She felt and saw intense sorrow and sadness, a whole multitude of emotions. She then saw the three of us taken to a place. According to Penny, "It was dark for a long time. We were traveling through clouds. When we arrived, I saw the three of us dressed in white, performing our favorite tasks. Carrie was in a field with children running around. I saw myself surrounded by lush plants. And then I saw you, Deanna, sitting on the ground as a wise teacher surrounded by adults."

Upon listening to both accounts, I could feel intense anger rise in my chest. Before expressing my sheer disappointment regarding my lack of experience, Carrie remembered an additional detail. She was told that we were experiencing "death, life, and healing." Annoyed, I shared with them the message I had received the prior week. I ran to my closet to grab my notebook and show them. Her message mirrored the exact message I had channeled. They were excited, and I was beyond livid. Truthfully, angry does not begin to explain the level of anguish I felt.

After they left the house, I paced back and forth. I grabbed my notebook in which I'd channeled the message the week before, stating that I, too, was supposed to experience this phenomenon. I proceeded to cook dinner, and afterward while taking a shower, I began to cry. I could not stop asking why this occurred. How could this be? I put all my trust and faith in this message. I was thoroughly disappointed, and my heart was broken. I spent a majority of the night on my knees trying to understand. Why would they tell me this and then prohibit my experience? The more I prayed for understanding, the more enraged I became. I truly felt betrayed. Some small part of me believed that my sight was going to be restored that day during that experience.

The next morning I tried to rationalize why I was prevented from having this experience. I succumbed to my negative cyclical reasoning and contemplated my self-worth. Was I being punished? Was I not a worthy candidate? This was truly a slippery slope, and the deeper I explored, the darker my thoughts became. I could feel the cold depths of my despair, and I did not want to pray again. After all, I had been praying and petitioning for help for five months with no visual results. I begged and pleaded my higher power for any explanation for clarity of some sort. This was the beginning of many emotional breakdowns.

I received a text message from Carrie in the afternoon the next day. She told me she was mad that I had not shared the same experience, and wondered why. Carrie is profoundly clairsentient. She revealed to me that she could feel the intensity of my sadness. I was relieved to hear and feel the depths of her empathy; it somehow minimized my sorrow. Penny, Carrie, and I met weekly. Although I wanted to see them and practice, I was still sad and even embarrassed from the previous week's visit. When they arrived, we sat on the floor and revisited their experiences to confirm the accuracy of my documentation. Upon finishing that discussion, Carrie asked aloud why I was not able to witness the previous event. A few minutes later she relayed the message: "There is another plan for you," she said. And although I felt relieved, I could not pretend the answer was at all satisfactory. I wondered, What could be better than seeing Heaven?

Over the course of the month we practiced the pyramid. As we sat down in the pyramid shape, we first rubbed our hands together to open our hand chakras. We protected ourselves, prayed, and then closed our eyes. I sat with my eyes closed, trying to imagine the large, three-dimensional diamond spinning in the middle of the three of us. As I held their hands, I could feel the power of their energy surge through me. Carrie released her hands from mine and Penny's about ten minutes after we began. She exchanged looks with Penny first and then back at me. She asked me, "Nothing? You saw nothing again?" The words pierced my heart like sharp blades. I responded, "No, nothing." Carrie shared her account of what just occurred: "I saw a vision of Jesus on the cross and heard him say that he has risen, and we will be there." Penny affirmed, "I saw Jesus as well, and he said that he has risen, and so will we." Tears filled our eyes and we were honored by the grace of God's love.

Carrie and Penny's gifts continued to grow over the months. While I loved helping them, I felt depressed afterward. I didn't truly know if I *was* helping them. My clairvoyance was still absent and so was my clairaudience. My emotions fluctuated daily, and the condition of my mental state was unpredictable. I was spending more time on my knees praying for help and guidance then I did standing up.

During our many readings, we were guided to take a trip to Mount Shasta. I was told I would meet my guide there. *Finally*, I thought. A miracle. It's strange to think about how much I relied on my first guide for so many answers in such a short period of time. I truly missed him and even found myself mourning him. He was such a beacon of light, laughter, and truth. I was beginning to feel as if I was being put through a test of inner faith and courage. I remember that at one miserably low point throughout the process, I miraculously heard one of my many guides tell me to please have enough faith in God, since he has so much faith in me. That voice also chastised me and declared, "Victimhood does not suit you." Perhaps I couldn't hear or see in order to begin trusting my inner voice and God without these gifts. Little did I discern that my guides had become a crutch. I relied so much on receiving answers directly from my guide and angels that I rarely sat down and asked my inner voice.

The trip to Mount Shasta was honestly not what I expected. Actually, I did not know what was to happen, except that I would finally meet my guide. Unfortunately, Penny could not make the trip, but a great friend of mine, Vivian, whom I was also teaching, accompanied Carrie and me on our drive to the mountain. My knowledge of the mystical aspects of the mountain was minimal. I knew that many spiritual seekers transverse the globe to visit this sacred place, and healing waters are said to flow by the mountain. I was aware of the stories of the ascended master occupying this mountain, but I did not know why *we* needed to be there.

We arrived at the mountain and found a small patch of grass to lay our blankets on. Sitting in this patch, we meditated and received messages about each other's lives and what was to come. I waited for my guide to appear, or at least call my name, but he made no appearance. Before leaving this mountain, we were told to make three wishes, which would be granted by the mountain. We stood facing the mountain and stated our wishes and left.

When we returned from Mount Shasta, I felt lost and completely impatient. Prior to this part of my journey, I never felt so impatient in all of my life. I was disappointed, again. Why didn't my guide step forward to meet me? What was happening to me? I was quick to anger and frequently carried frustration in my mind and body. I did not see myself moving forward with psychic development, but instead I saw myself taking countless steps back. I fought myself day and night. There were moments when I cried nonstop, pounding my fists into the wall anywhere I could, really. And other days, I cried in prayer for help to see the situation differently. Some days I did all right. But the truth is, most days I wanted to give up.

Regardless, I never gave up. Penny became very busy and no longer practiced with Carrie and me. I continued to teach Carrie and my dear friend Vivian to expand their clairvoyance and clairaudience. I led them through many guided meditations and shared specific techniques; I was truly committed to teaching Vivian and Carrie everything I'd learned. I began to receive repetitive messages from Carrie's guide that it was time to begin spreading awareness. Angel numbers 999 and 911 frequently appeared on license plates, on billboards, and in phone numbers. The angels were urging me to start my life purpose now! I wasn't even sure what that was. Carrie received the recurring message that I was to start teaching others what I'd learned and to write a book about it.

Initially, I was extremely hesitant. What did I really have to contribute? What have I learned, exactly? I never really took an inventory of the depth of my acquired knowledge. Additionally, my sight and sound were still incredibly limited, and I battled the idea of writing a book from the start. I did love to write, but I sort of felt out of commission. I struggled to understand what I could teach. And would anyone believe me? I didn't see myself as a figure of authority on anything. I temporarily shelved the messages from the angels and her guide.

Although I tried to avoid the angel's messages, I began to see the number 899 on cars, T-shirts, and billboards. From Doreen Virtue's *Angel Numbers*, 899 means: "Let go of any tendencies to procrastinate about your spiritual career and divine mission, and know that the sooner you take guided action, the sooner you'll experience the bliss and abundance that accompanies your purpose."[1]

I acknowledged the message but still refused to write. It took a message from the angels through Carrie and my sister to really help me believe that I could indeed write a book that would be of help to people who were on the same path or ready to shift the direction of their life.

I became increasingly concerned about writing a book on this topic, given that I had not been able to successfully channel in quite some time and was worried that my experiences and methods were questionable. After all, how can others follow you if you cannot demonstrate? I posed this question to my guide. Through my sister, he told me to trust in God's plan and to simply surrender. I struggled for many months to write. I was very doubtful about the process. It took three years to learn exactly why I was going through this period of dormancy. As expressed by my guide in the simplest form, "There is a season for everything, and this is a season of rest, studying, and making my dreams come true." I spent the last year taking classes, practicing, and teaching, but I did not rest. Instead, by dulling my other senses, I was being led to rest and conserve energy in some form or fashion. According to the angels, I was giving so many readings and channeling numerous messages for friends and family that all my energy was being expelled to help others, but unbeknown to me, I was creating an energy imbalance in my life. As such, I was desperately in need of energy conservation and restoration. It was as if I was forcibly being placed into a period of hibernation.

During this time, too, I was to study and establish a foundation of knowledge, which I was doing, but it did not remain my central focus. Lastly, I was being encouraged to follow my dreams of writing and teaching. Although I viewed this cycle of my life as lacking any significant growth, it was anything but. It took some time to really understand and accept that there are periods of growth and periods of rest and silence; this work requires a lot of patience. It is important to inform you that you will experience periods of silence and restoration, since you must balance giving and receiving, the expelling of energy and its conservation.

Learning to surrender is a crucial part of this process. The word "surrender" is tossed around in spiritual circles, but what does this really mean? In my experience, surrender involves relinquishing control of a situation and trusting in God's plan for your life. As humans in this three-dimensional world, it is frightening to relinquish our roles as the puppet masters of our life. Upon entrance into this world, we are taught to methodically outline our life plan with clear routes intended to result in our happiness. In other words, we submit to the notion that we know best. However, when we are asked to shift into a state of surrender, we have the opportunity to witness the miraculous unfoldment of our lives given by the divine architect, thus admitting the limited state of our perception and awareness. In my case, surrender involved releasing my anger over the lack of control over the development of my gifts or lack thereof.

Furthermore, surrendering requires having faith in God that your current situation serves a higher purpose, which you may not currently understand. When we are experiencing a down cycle in our lives, it is easier to sink into our personal plight of victimhood. We assume that our dark obstacles, internal traumas, and external crises are intentionally commissioned on high as injurious tactics to prevent our success and happiness. But to surrender means that we willingly hand over our perception and interpretation of why those challenges occur. Moreover, to surrender is to trust that while your dreams might not be manifesting according to *your* expectations, or if you are experiencing delays or roadblocks, everything will occur for your highest good at the right time. In an attempt to surrender, I finally sat down and let the words flow.

CHAPTER 9

Christianity Revisited: The Bible, Jesus, and Psychic Development

Earlier in this book, I spoke about my experiences in the Christian church and how they promoted and instituted fear-based consciousness within my being. However, as you have probably detected, I have chosen not to dismiss Christianity altogether. While I personally found some of the tenets composing this religion to inaugurate a sense of fear, lack, and poverty consciousness (and here I am speaking specifically about my experiences and acknowledge that there are multiple denominations that interpret the Bible differently), I was encouraged to go back and revisit the teachings of Jesus and their relationship to psychic development and the evolution of the soul. In the New Age community, Jesus is considered a great Ascended Master. This means that during his incarnation, he remembered and reclaimed his true identity as one with the *all that is*, or God, and embodied that consciousness, in this case called "Christ consciousness," as he occupied this Earth plane. This remembrance was exemplified in his complete faith in his unity with God, which enabled him, without doubt, to perform what we consider to be "miracles." Additionally, this reclamation allowed him to learn and teach eternal spiritual truths. To many in the Christian community, this appears to bastardize who Jesus was, his messages, and his miracles and even to demote his status as savior and son of God. However, throughout my revisitation of Jesus in the New Testament, I personally found Jesus to have been a master metaphysical teacher, scholar, and divine healer.

I remember as a child and teenager that the "message" of Jesus was "the cross." There was no message about psychic or mystical development. In essence, Jesus came here to die for our sins, and if we claimed him as our true savior, then we were saved from the pit of Hell. I further remember thinking that this man was crucified to save me from all the sins I had yet to commit, and save me from my inherently sinful nature. As I studied the gospels, I wondered why God sent his only son to planet Earth to die in order to save me from my sins. That actually sounded quite awful. I further pondered why it is that we are so fascinated with this message. In one sense, this "message of the cross" institutes a sense of guilt. But also this message promotes the idea that we, as spirits, and humans here on Earth, are absolved of our actions as long as we claim him as our savior. This message did not resonate with me. Was this really the message that this wondrous spirit came here to teach? I further wondered how I could reconcile my new beliefs and experiences with Jesus's teachings.

As I explored Matthew, Mark, Luke, and John, I identified what I found to be some of the most profound teachings by this master metaphysical teacher. I believe that these teachings were essentially about the awakening and transformation of the soul, or "psychic development."

1. Love: In many of his teachings, Jesus emphasizes the necessity of love because it facilitates the activation and metamorphosis of the soul. For example, Jesus tells his students in the book of Matthew, "*But I say unto you, Love your enemies, bless them that curse you, do good to them that hate you, and pray for them which despitefully use you, and persecute you.*"[1] In Luke we find the same iteration:

> *But I say unto you which hear, Love your enemies, do good to them which hate you, Bless them that curse you, and pray for them which despitefully*

use you. And unto him that smiteth thee on the one cheek offer also the other; and him that taketh away thy cloak forbid not to take thy coat also. Give to every man that asketh of thee; and of him that taketh away thy goods ask them not again.[2]

When asked by his apostles about the greatest commandment, Jesus responds,"*Thou shalt love the Lord thy God with all thy heart, and with all thy soul, and with all thy mind. This is the first and great commandment. And the second is like unto it, Thou shalt love thy neighbour as thyself. On these two commandments hang all the laws and the prophets.*"[3]

Repeatedly in the book of John, Jesus tells his disciples to love one another.[4] This is because by loving one another equally, we processually awaken, remember, and reclaim our true divine heritage and identity, whose natural state operates beyond the boundaries of this physical reality. As we embody our true state of being through self-love, love of God, and love of our neighbors, our connection to divine mind and our access to celestial knowledge, power, and wisdom are strengthened. Loving is a godly force that purifies and unlocks the eye of our hearts, through which all development and transformation occur. Christ reiterated in his Sermon on the Mount that the pure at heart will see God.[5] And to see God is to know God, meaning that through acts of unconditional love, we come to embody, learn, and witness the profound transformative power of God's love, whereby all "limitations" of this world fall away. One such limitation includes that of blocked sight. As our hearts are purified, we naturally develop spiritual perception or the sight of the soul.

Love is the most powerful force in the universe and unifies all spirits. This empowering energy allows us to work together as a force of light to heal and collectively progress. It is the true Alpha and Omega. Jesus promoted love-based thinking, which was much unlike his predecessors. This type of thinking is very important for the development of one's gifts, because all creation and development happens at the level of positive and love-based thinking and through an open heart.

2. Reaping and Sowing: Jesus also teaches about the concept of reaping and sowing, not because it is God's will to punish us, but because it is a dynamic and just law of the universe.[6] There are multiple reasons why he stresses this law. First, because the universe is maintained by balance and harmony. In order to maintain balance, what is given must be received in like and kind. This means that if we perform an act that is unconditionally loving, we too will experience unconditional love. However, if we create fear and pain, then we too will reap that in like and kind out of complete fairness, not judgment or punishment.

In Mark, Matthew, and Luke, Jesus states the following:

Hearken; Behold, there went out a sower to sow: And it came to pass, as he sowed, some fell by the way side, and the fowls of the air came and devoured it up. And some fell on stony ground, where it had not much Earth; and immediately it sprang up, because it had no depth of Earth: But when the sun was up, it was scorched; and because it had no root, it withered away. And some fell among thorns, and the thorns grew up, and choked it, and it yielded no fruit. And other fell on good ground, and did yield fruit that sprang up and increased; and brought forth, some thirty, and some sixty, and some an hundred.[7]

The seed is representative of our actions and thought forms. If we act without love and compassion, then those actions will be received in the same form; in a similar vein, if we think without love, possessed with negative thought forms, then the result will be negative and loveless. There are natural consequences to our thoughts and actions. Jesus is stating a profound spiritual truth to his disciples, which is essentially the law of cause and effect, occurring at the level of the mind and even the heart, where all creation and transformation occur. You can receive only what you are willing to give mentally, spiritually, and physically.

This law of reaping and sowing is important for those wanting to access and develop the greater gifts. In the Bible we are told, "*Keep thy heart with all diligence; for out of it are the issues of life.*"[8] While on Earth, we experience the physical manifestation of the condition of our hearts. A closed and unforgiving heart is a blocked and unreceptive vessel, and an open heart gives and receives love naturally, which easily allows for the spiritual transmission of God's love and healing. To develop your gifts, again, you must have an open heart and give love unconditionally to others; upon doing this, then the eye of the heart will open and divine knowledge will be available as God speaks to us through our hearts. If you have created a personal reality of lovelessness, unforgiveness, and negativity, then it will be difficult to access your psychic abilities, given the law of reaping and sowing.

This divine law of reaping and sowing is God's reality, and thus it is ours. Jesus reminds his students, "*Trust in the reality that is God's, where his laws (his words) are the truth, the way and the life. Live on these, not the material world that you see."*[9]

Why is this important for psychic development? This particular knowledge helps us transcend the limitations we experience at the level of the mind in the three-dimensional world, which prevents our development. During our development, many of us possess thoughts of doubt, lack, and failure, and this becomes our own personal reality and experience. The universe gives us only what we have produced in our mind. If we choose to trust in God's reality, or his laws, then we find that when we reach for higher vibratory, or loving and positive thoughts about our psychic abilities, our gifts will actually blossom and flourish. It is at this juncture where we access and operate within the dimension of truth.

3. Faith: In the first four gospels of the New Testament, or synoptic gospels, Jesus reiterates the importance of having faith and reminds us what faith and conviction can do. Jesus is widely recognized for performing several healing miracles, whose success he attributes to his absolute faith in God, and the faith of those who are sick. In the book of Matthew, Jesus raises a girl from the dead and heals a sickly woman. After healing the sick woman, he tells her, *"thy faith hath made thee whole."*[10] In Mark, Jesus heals a blind man and again tells him, *"thy faith hath made thee whole."*[11] As reflected in the gospels, Jesus further emphasizes that it truly is the person's undeniable faith in their own ability to be healed that allows it to be so. It is their complete belief in divine healing. This belief occurs again at the level of the mind. He repeatedly states, *"Your faith has made you well."* Therefore, lack of faith may prevent one from experiencing divine healing and even developing their abilities to heal others. In Matthew, Jesus heals a boy possessed by a demon. His disciples ask him why they could not do it themselves, and Jesus responds, *"Because of your unbelief: for verily I say unto you, If ye have faith as a grain of mustard seed, ye shall say unto this mountain, Remove hence to yonder place; and it shall remove; and nothing shall be impossible unto you."*[12]

Jesus teaches us to have unshakable faith about who and what we are, which is pure divine love and unlimited potential as children of God. What he asks us to do is know thyself, or remember our true divinity, and that we derive from the unlimited source of *all that is.* Furthermore, we are asked to have faith, or a true knowingness about our identity, which is boundless and unlimited and part of a unified force. Jesus encourages us to operate within that dimension of pure faith and trust where anything is truly possible. This includes the ability to embody psychic gifts. Faith operates here as an active force of knowingness and elicits manifestation. It is an expression of your confidence that you, as spirit, are unified continuously with source and thus have source energy (God) being channeled through you consistently, which enables you to do the "impossible."

It is our faith in the knowledge of who we are that helps us develop our psychic abilities. In orthodox Christianity, there is the concept of blind faith, which implies a faith without seeing or even knowing. The faith espoused by Jesus encompasses a knowingness. This act of faith allows you, with conviction, to perform miracles such as heal the sick and see through the third eye or hear with spiritual ears. The type of faith Jesus refers to is akin to building your house on rock, not on sand. In Matthew, Jesus tells us:

Therefore whosoever heareth these sayings of mine, and doeth them, I will liken him unto a wise man, which built his house upon a rock: And the rain descended, and the floods came, and the winds blew, and beat upon that house; and it fell not: for it was founded upon a rock. And every one that heareth these sayings of mine, and doeth them not, shall be likened unto a foolish man, which built his house upon the sand: And the rain descended, and the floods came, and the winds blew, and beat upon that house; and it fell: and great was the fall of it.[13]

Either at the outset of your development or even during, you must strengthen your faith and believe that you are indeed innately gifted with otherworldly abilities.

4. Forgiveness: Forgiveness is a crucial part of psychic development because it heals and purifies our heart, which is necessary to perform psychic work. Jesus emphasizes this healing force throughout the gospels. In Matthew, Jesus states, *"For if ye forgive men their trespasses, your Heavenly Father will also forgive you: But if ye forgive not men their trespasses, neither will your Father forgive your trespasses."*[14]

Jesus simply reiterates the message of the law of balance, reaping and sowing, and the golden rule, which extends naturally throughout the universe. Through forgiveness, we express and demonstrate our true divinity as Jesus did. As we forgive others for their mistakes, we extend our healing love and remember who and what we are. Implied is the recognition here that we, too, make errors along the way while we learn, and our ability to forgive heals our own heart and strengthens our spirit connection to the creator, who is all that is. We teach what we best need to learn, and as we teach forgiveness by doing it, we reinforce the lesson of forgiveness in our own minds and hearts through conscious practice. In the gospels, Jesus protects an adulterous woman by stating, "*So when they continued asking him, he lifted up himself, and said unto them, He that is without sin among you, let him first cast a stone at her.*"[15]

This lesson is ultimately about forgiving our judgments regarding a person's decisions and actions. Forgiveness naturally contains miraculous alchemical properties that convert density into weightlessness and darkness into light. Forgiveness, and even acceptance, ultimately brings healing to the heart and peace to the mind, both of which are prerequisites for the development and maintenance of the gifts of spirit.

5. Identity: By awakening your psychic self, you will remember your true identity, which is always connected to God and is the light of the world. Jesus states this in Matthew 5:14. He says this in a literal sense because you truly are the light; we all are. We are sent here as representatives of the creator force, God, the *all that is*, to bring light and love and to express that here individually. Jesus insists that we not hide our light but shine it brightly for the world! In Matthew he states:

Ye are the light of the world. A city that is set on a hill cannot be hid. Neither do men light a candle, and put it under a bushel, but on a candlestick; and it giveth light unto all that are in the house. Let your light so shine before men, that they may see your good works, and glorify your Father which is in Heaven. Think not that I am come to destroy the law, or the prophets: I am not come to destroy, but to fulfill.[16]

Jesus asks us not to deny our true selves or our greatness. By demonstrating our light daily, we help others remember their true nature, and our actions reinforce who we are in our very own mind.

We are eternally unified with the creator force and comprise one loving energy. In the book of Romans, Paul affirms, "*I am persuaded, that neither death, nor life, nor angels, nor principalities, nor powers, nor things present, nor things to come, Nor height, nor depth, nor any other creature, shall be able to separate us from the love of God, which is in Christ Jesus our Lord.*"[17]

We are never separate from source and the love of God. No thing or time or space separates us from the love of God. And this love abides not only within the spirit of Jesus, but within all of us. God's love, which is the source of all things, flows through us as channels endlessly and eternally; all we need do is remember and access this. Our true self, our "God self," "higher self," or even "spirit self," is unified with *all that is.*

It is reiterated in 1 Corinthians:

> *For as the body is one, and hath many members, and all the members of that one body, being many, are one body: so also is Christ. For by one Spirit are we all baptized into one body, whether we be Jews or Gentiles, whether we be bond or free; and have been all made to drink into one Spirit. For the body is not one member, but many. If the foot shall say, Because I am not the hand, I am not of the body; is it therefore not of the body? And if the ear shall say, Because I am not the eye, I am not of the body; is it therefore not of the body? If the whole body were an eye, where were the hearing? If the whole were hearing, where were the smelling? But now hath God set the members every one of them in the body, as it hath pleased him. And if they were all one member, where were the body?*
>
> *But now are they many members, yet but one body. And the eye cannot say unto the hand, I have no need of thee: nor again the head to the feet, I have no need of you. Nay, much more those members of the body, which seem to be more feeble, are necessary: And those members of the body, which we think to be less honourable, upon these we bestow more abundant honour; and our uncomely parts have more abundant comeliness. For our comely parts have no need: but God hath tempered the body together, having given more abundant honour to that part which lacked. That there should be no schism in the body; but that the members should have the same care one for another. And whether one member suffer, all the members suffer with it; or one member be honoured, all the members rejoice with it. Now ye are the body of Christ, and members in particular. And God hath set some in the church, first apostles, secondarily prophets, thirdly teachers, after that miracles, then gifts of healings, help, governments, diversities of tongues. Are all apostles? Are all prophets? are all teachers? Are all workers of miracles? Have all the gifts of healing? Do all speak with tongues? Do all interpret? But covet earnestly the best gifts: and yet shew I unto you a more excellent way.*[18]

Knowing that we are truly a composite of the unified divine mind, or "Body of Christ," is imperative to the evolution of the psychic self. This tells us that we are always connected and that God's energy flows through our spirit. This means that we, too, as spiritual beings having a physical experience, have the natural ability to access what already lies inside us. Here is another revelation of truth about our psychic self. We need to be aware that we are not accessing information that is separated from us, or external to us, but instead is natural since we exist as part of the "Body of Christ," which encompasses the greater gifts.

6. The Gifts of Spirit: Jesus came to teach us immutable divine truths about ourselves and the laws of God's reality, which is the only reality and is unlimited by the five senses. He further teaches us how to transform ourselves spiritually by helping us reclaim our divine personhood, which consists of unlimited potential and spiritual gifts. In 1 Corinthians the apostle Paul tells us:

Wherefore I give you to understand, that no man speaking by the Spirit of God calleth Jesus accursed: and that no man can say that Jesus is the Lord, but by the Holy Ghost. Now there are diversities of gifts, but the same Spirit. And there are differences of administrations, but the same Lord. And there are diversities of operations, but it is the same God which worketh all in all. But the manifestation of the Spirit is given to every man to profit withal. For to one is given by the Spirit the word of wisdom; to another the word of knowledge by the same Spirit; To another faith by the same Spirit; to another the gifts of healing by the same Spirit; To another the working of miracles; to another prophecy; to another discerning of spirits; to another divers kinds of tongues; to another the interpretation of tongues: But all these worketh that one and the selfsame Spirit, dividing to every man severally as he will.[19]

It is apparent that distributed through the Body of Christ, or existing within the unified divine mind and heart, are multiple gifts, which we carry within ourselves. Some of us are gifted with the ability to heal, and others with the ability to prophesize; some can speak in tongues, and some have access to illumined wisdom and knowledge—all of which are used to help spirits here on this Earthly plane.

Upon the revisitation of all things Jesus and the Bible, I have come to understand, as many already do, that these gifts have been ever present. Time has been a witness to many prophets claiming to have had visions and prophetic dreams; these prophets even profess to have heard disembodied voices and to have seen apparitions of varying sorts. There have been healers and those who speak in tongues. Nowhere is it declared that these abilities are no longer available or even present today. Why is there an assumption that the creator would suddenly discontinue the distribution of the gifts of spirit upon the conclusion of the Bible? Therefore, all of us have these innate abilities manifesting in form at some level, only to be harnessed and developed. Even Paul encourages us to desire the greater gifts.

Overall, Jesus's message was positive, supportive, and encouraging. He teaches us about the power of love and forgiveness as a unifying and healing force. He further encourages us to have faith, which is a reflection of your confidence in God and affirmation of the presence of God's power and truth. He teaches us about the golden rule and even about the law of cause and effect. Jesus demonstrated how to consciously transform the soul through love, forgiveness, faith, and remembering our unified identity. This must happen at the level of the mind with love-based thinking and also with an open heart, which is what Jesus reaffirms through his words and actions. These principles create an open and clear channel for the expression of your gifts to be used in collective healing.

Furthermore, it is important to mention that in Christianity, Jesus is portrayed as a flawless human being, already spiritually evolved; this creates for us an image that is seemingly impossible to become or even aspire to. However, Jesus, too, had to overcome the challenges, or illusions and weaknesses of the human self, and transform himself by the same laws and principles he espouses in his teachings. No one is exempt. On a few occasions, for example in the book of Matthew, we find Jesus upset, sad, and even crying, displaying human emotions of fear and suffering during his individual challenges.[20] We also find Jesus praying in Matthew 26:36–39, 42; Luke 6:12; and Mark 1:35. His journey is a demonstration that awakening the true self, or psychic self, is indeed an emotional process similar to our own. However, by applying the exact same principles and methods, we too have the potential to be like Jesus in like and kind. In a Christian mindset, Jesus and his abilities appear inaccessible, or "special"; however, we all are the sons of God made in the image of our creator, and nothing is denied to any of us—all of us are equal.

CHAPTER 10

Spiritual Growth

One of the intentions for this book is to help everyone, especially current and former Christians, feel comfortable and safe opening up to their gifts. Traditional biblical scripture condemns any form of psychic work and thus engenders an immense sense of fear upon those who wish to explore the nature of their spiritual talents. I hope that my journey navigating through unknown territories of the psychic world operates as a comforting device as you dismantle the burden of Christian guilt. Initially, you will experience many roadblocks as you begin your pilgrimage. For most, the initial challenge will be your willingness to believe something new. Many people think they are open to change, but truthfully most are resistant and uncomfortable with the idea of having to surrender their attachments to a particular belief system. To take this step, you must open your heart and your mind to purge old systems of thought. You must allow yourself to confront your existing beliefs and surrender what no longer serves you. In other words, bring your darkness to the light for healing. Those who find themselves at the beginning of this journey are usually at a crossroads in their faith. If you've consistently had "psychic" or unexplained experiences, chances are you've spent some moments attributing this to the Devil or some dark entity. It can be quite a challenge relinquishing this belief, and it takes much trust and faith in your higher power and in your own intuition.

Unfortunately, it is not that easy to transition into a new belief system, and it does not occur overnight. Your guides and angels are completely aware of this. It took many years and methods of conditioning your mind to its current state; therefore, you need an army of light to help dismantle your current patterns. Remember, the psychic journey is about the continuous expansion of the mind and the heart. As you progress on this path, you will encounter new philosophies, theories, and beliefs that will challenge your long-held perceptions and disrupt your very own system of thought. The purpose of this is to slowly deconstruct rigid and uncompromising mental patterns that paralyze your vision and understanding of your identity and the consciousness and connection of *all that is*. At some juncture of your pilgrimage, you may be strongly encouraged to reevaluate your interpretation and experience of reality. By doing so, you then become privy to your existing mental barriers to truth; as a consequence, you will understand the origin of these barriers (which are beliefs) as well as implement methods to dismantle them. This allows for a shift in your perception and a subsequent energetic, mental, and emotional transformation. The ultimate goal is to alchemize the mind from frequencies of negativity and fear to those of positivity and love. These particular shifts in thought directly affect the realm and evolution of the heart. The expansion and rehabilitation of the mind, because of these particular shifts in perception from negative to positive, facilitate pathways of healing in the heart by removing blocks and reinserting the presence of love, the true healer. For the psychic, a healed heart grants clear vision.

Our egos are so grandiose that they will actively challenge new ideas and different ways of thinking and believing. You will relapse many times as you navigate this path, primarily due to Christian guilt. I must reiterate here that I am not advocating a complete dismissal of all Christian beliefs in which you subscribe; however, know that over time, your complete acceptance and belief in particular scriptures will resurface and protest this transition.

The weight of this guilt can be crushing, since a majority of Christians are raised to believe that acting in "opposition" to God is akin to sinning, which results in punishment. Sojourning onto a path that deviates from traditional Christian tenants will no doubt instill within you a major sense of fear. It is at this crossroad where you must pray for guidance and take the necessary steps. Know that you are not alone on your pilgrimage. Be aware that the whole universe is watching your personal awakening and is invested in your enlightenment. This is a very powerful statement, and it is a true one. My guides and angels reiterated that it takes only one match to light an entire room of darkness. Meaning that if one person opens their heart and their mind to the love that is God, which encompasses all truth and knowledge, they become the conduit to carry and dispense pure light and healing wisdom of the creator to rehabilitate the world. This is not an independent journey, and a brigade of light will guide you, teach you, and illuminate you to ultimately be of assistance to the world. Remember that the path and the destination of the psychic is not self-contained; it is for the benefit of all light beings.

Along this path you will encounter doubts about your worthiness. As told in biblical scripture, we are inherently sinful; however, in truth, we are perfect. At various periods during this path I felt completely unworthy as a human being, given my past mistakes and negative thoughts. Who was I to correspond with the angels of God? Who was I to receive such gifts? Remember though that Jesus tells us, "*Unto you it is given to know the mystery of the kingdom of God.*"[1]

I cannot stress enough how much of this journey is built on faith and trust. As I stated earlier, faith involves a knowingness. It is a revelation of the magnitude of your certainty and confidence in God. Given the obvious fluctuations you will experience as you awaken, your faith as a child of God will be required. Trust is an additional component of this journey. It is essential to trust that we are being guided every step of the way even when the pathway is not clear. We must also trust our own inner voice and, above all, trust that any direction we take will be used by the universe or God to serve our highest good.

While this may sound redundant, the point of this work is to learn how to trust your own gifts and intuition. A close friend of mine has the phenomenal gift of clairaudience; however, she struggles to believe the messages given to her and instead continually seeks out other psychics for answers, which occasionally end up mirroring her own. Opening up to the psychic self requires great trust and confidence in the *all that is*, which is the voice of your intuition. As you begin, there will be much confusion, misinterpretation, and great surprises as well. This is the true process, the unfolding of your spirit.

There are times when I experienced the expansion of my gifts and times when they were dormant or less accessible. Be aware that this, too, is a part of the learning process and the expansion of self. At one point during my dormant period, my guide told me to be like the rose. It took me a while to understand what that meant. I have been told that if we look outside our windows we will find the answers to many of our questions in life. Upon reflection, I understood that our lives mirror the life cycle of a rose. First, a seed is planted and then nurtured with warm sun and water. After some time, the rose bud appears and is covered by a green leaflike structure, called a sepal, until it is ready for reproduction. Once the sepals expand, the flower begins to bloom. Like many flowers, roses grow and bloom during spring and summer and then wither away in the fall and winter cycles, only to bloom and renew themselves in the springtime again. Like the rose, the spring and summer were major periods of growth and expansion. My gifts were fully nurtured and protected by the sun, or god-source energy. By putting my gifts into practice, they expanded.

Like the rose in the fall and winter cycles, my gifts experienced a dormant period, which was a period of hibernation and self-reflection. It is important to know that this cycle is the actual process. Spiritual growth is not a linear journey. There are many lessons we have to learn and relearn to ensure understanding. This is the same for psychic development.

There is a grand misconception that if we are on this path we get to bypass life's major obstacles and hurdles. While I've opened myself up to spirit in mind and heart, this does not mean I no longer experience life's challenges. In fact, the challenge has become how to maneuver these speed bumps with the knowledge I have acquired. It is mistaken to think that once you've opened those channels of communication, you have access to all of life's answers. In truth, you will be provided an objective perspective to your rational, ego-based thinking. But while this is so, no one and no thing can tell you what to do. All decisions and choices are yours.

We are constantly in a state of spiritual maturation. Every step on our journey is a lesson to be learned and applied. In the field of psychic development, every small step helps fully craft and strengthen your trust in your intuition and psychic abilities. As your gifts develop, you will learn how to heal yourself and transmit healing light to others and even enlighten those within your field of action.

Family Acceptance

In my early twenties, my father began to question his own religious beliefs. I will not say this was a crisis, but an exploration beyond the doctrine of our church. Unbeknown to my father, his own quest of self-discovery planted the seed of my spiritual introspection. If he had not been brave enough to question his own truth and isolate it from the truth of the church, I would not have had the courage to address and investigate my very own.

When I first began to channel, I was worried about sharing the information I began receiving from the divine. Both of my parents were at the point in their lives when they, too, wanted to find a better way, a more joyful and loving way of being in the world beyond what they learned in church. I took a leap of faith when I shared the messages with them. And they responded with so much love and acceptance as the messages resonated deep within their hearts. For them, it was a movement toward healing.

I realize that this type of response, in reality, is uncharacteristic and that most people who choose to share the experiences of their spiritual evolution are met with skepticism, criticism, judgment, fear, and even anger. It is hard enough coming from virtually no religious background, but even more so having been raised in a family that is devout. People may assume that you believe you are more special or that you have something they do not. They may react with fear simply because they, themselves, do not understand.

I am aware of the major arguments against what I deem to be spiritual mysticism or what is simply known as psychic work. For Christians, this is quite difficult to digest, given the magnitude of biblical condemnation. Many who privately practice and commit themselves to embracing their divine mystical heritage find it challenging to share their knowledge and even to publicly demonstrate. Most would rather practice in private rather than be branded as a witch, sorcerer, cheater, liar, fake, and Devil worshiper. And while we fear losing our family ties and their approval, we must be brave to share our stories and our knowledge to bring light to this world. We need fear nothing. As light workers, I was told, our courage and confidence in God are required.

Again, on a personal note, I was beyond blessed to have parents and a sister who supported my journey and experiences. However, like most of you, I too have family members who do not necessarily approve of how I communicate and receive messages and guidance and how I practice overall. Additionally, some do not believe me because I no longer attend a formal church. Truthfully, my first instinct emanating from my ego was to "prove them wrong." But my heart said meet them with the power of love.

Throughout this journey I learned that we pick our families prior to our Earthly incarnation. As teachers and learners of God, we each have valuable lessons to teach and learn from our relationships with one another. Familial relationships are more commonly our most difficult ones to maneuver as we journey through life on this Earth plane. Our parents establish our habitus filled with their personal belief systems, which were most likely structured by their parents' belief system. You are, in essence, indoctrinated into a way of living and even responding. Sometimes in these relationships, we struggle to be ourselves, to be independent, and to develop our identity, and we also are wounded at times and we hurt as well. These are deeply complex relationships in which we constantly learn and teach lessons to each other, and it can be messy. It can be very challenging to share your spiritual journey if your family's belief system is deeply rooted in a strict, inflexible doctrine. Although it may be difficult to view it this way, by opening up to very resistant and perhaps unsupportive families, we are learning the valuable lesson of love and forgiveness, while simultaneously sharing and teaching our knowledge.

Transitional Changes

As you reclaim your abilities and commit yourself to developing them, you will notice a variety of changes internally and externally. As my guide Orion told me, "Changes from within always bring about changes without." These changes will manifest through adjustments in friends and relationships. As the saying goes, show me your friends, and I will tell you who you are. As you begin to move throughout your journey, you will likely experience synchronicity in your life and attract a like-minded community. Within the past few years, people have become aware of the law of attraction, the idea that "like attracts like" or "birds of a feather flock together." In simplistic terms, this law states that people who are similar, in like and kind, attract each other. What does this mean for you as you navigate your journey? This means that as you spiritually grow, through prayer, meditation, and devoted practice, you change your internal frequency. Your thoughts shift, your perceptions shift, and you begin to naturally attract like-minded people. These people will likely be navigating the road less traveled that you yourself are on. This is truly a beautiful gift from our creator. As we learn to navigate the unclear waters of this journey, we attract fellow seekers who will help us, and we too get the privilege to help them. Although we may experience struggles with the acceptance of family and close friends, the universe also supplies us with support and love.

What happens as you attract those who are seeking like you? Naturally those in your life who do not serve your highest good are in some way removed. This is not to say that you have become superior in some way. It is simply that you have replaced an old way of being with a new one, which no longer complements the beliefs you once held. This obviously affects your relationships with people in your life. For example, let's say that you previously inhabited a mindset that was frequently negative, and that your friends, too, were negative. Once you embark consciously on a journey of shifting your thoughts and your perception to a more positive outlook, it is likely that your "negative" friends will seek "approval" and agreement with their thoughts of negativity, which you will no longer provide. They will likely seek it elsewhere. Many people experience this phenomenon as they progress through their journey.

In my life, I noticed that the more I studied, prayed, meditated, and practiced developing my abilities, I attracted similar people who were doing the same. This even occurred at my job, of all places. I met a few coworkers who were also studying the same books and interested in similar activities. As I actively changed my thoughts, beliefs, and everyday practices, so too I noticed that I was surrounded by people who supported this mindful evolution.

Moving Forward

Many students have asked, Where do I begin? How do I move forward onto this psychic path? The ultimate consideration at the beginning of this journey should be your intention. Intentionality is the most important part of this work. Reflect on *why* you want to develop your gifts and how you want to contribute. Always remember that your gifts are not your own; they are to heal the collective. Document these and speak to your higher power about how you would best like to serve. Pray and ask God, the angels, your spirit guide, or your higher power to guide you to a book or author in alignment with your purpose. Rest assured they *will* find a way to get your attention.

While you may feel ready to transition onto a new path, the universe will require that you make some minor, sometimes major, adjustments in your current lifestyle and way of being. At the start of this journey, you will be required to purge what no longer serves you in your life, and the universe will willingly meet your request for change by gently modifying certain aspects of your life that are in need of recalibration. This means that your current way of operating, including your thoughts, emotions, and actions, must undergo some form of ablution. It is necessary to shed the current self for the revelation of the true self. Purification is required first, and then healing must occur. Personally, when I began this work, I was a very negative thinker. Given my life experiences, I always expected the worst, and indeed I got the worst. This obviously needed to be changed and required deep introspection and forgiveness work. Through forgiveness, self-acceptance, dedicated study, prayer, meditation, and much faith and trust, I was guided to slowly and processually shed that beloved persona. Now, do not believe I am suddenly a positive thinker. Absolutely not. But what I did do was invite the divine mind to consistently interact and intervene with my own to aid in the purification of my thoughts. This remains a *daily* practice and takes much commitment and devotion. The negative self that took over thirty years to create is slowly being dismantled.

The heart, too, must be purified. This usually requires forgiveness work on your part, primarily forgiveness of the self to open your heart. You cannot perform psychic work with a closed and unforgiving heart. Once your heart begins to heal and open, you then become a prime vessel for reception of your spiritual talents. Be aware that your spiritual team will guide you forward through every twist and turn. By the time you are at this stage, you will already have a good understanding of how you best wish to serve, which always parallels how God intends to work through you. Always extend gratitude for your gifts and use them wisely.

Maintaining Your Faith

In the *Merriam-Webster Dictionary*, faith is defined as (1) belief and trust in loyalty to God and (2) firm belief in something for which there is no proof.[2] On this particular path, your faith will repeatedly be tested. There is a general assumption that once you turn your life over to God, or seek the psychic path, your own Red Sea will neatly part, and you will be miraculously and easily delivered to the promised land. Although the promised land does exist, the journey there will be riddled with what appears to be an insurmountable and endless obstacle course with hurdles, twists, and turns. This is why maintaining your faith and your trust in God's plan is so important. You will need the words of God to carry you from one course to the next. In Romans it is written that *"faith comes by hearing and hearing by the word of God."*[3]

These "words of God" on the psychic path, or even the Christian path, contain the "still small voice" that is within us.[4] In other words, listening to your intuition to guide you step by step as God speaks to your spirit individually. At times it will appear as if your world if crashing down around you and swallowing you whole, which often accompanies a deep transformation onto the path of the psychic ministry. For some, major disruptions in your life will cause you to think that you are being punished by God for seeking differently. Nevertheless, what you may not be able to discern at the time is that during your pursuit for understanding the truth of your identity, which comprises the psychic ministry, all blocks to love must be removed.

Your faith is an expression of your confidence in God and the laws of God's reality. In Hebrews it is written that *"now faith is the assurance of things hoped for, the conviction of things not seen."*[5] Your faith is predicated on your ability to look past the challenges in your life, or beyond the three-dimensional plane, to see into the reality of God's laws of love, attraction, karma, and the law of one, and to believe and trust that they are really immutable. During your expedition it will seem as if you are alone, walking in darkness, but have the confidence that God, or *all that is*, has confidence in you to heal and be fearless. Each step you take forward, even if you fall, is a reflection of your belief not only in the unseen, but in the knowable.

Throughout this journey, it may appear as if I have moved away from Christianity altogether. This is far from the truth. This journey has actually brought me closer with Jesus and strengthened my relationship with him. While I no longer adhere to the belief that Jesus is my savior in the way traditional Christians believe, I have the blessing of working with him as a student to learn and apply his teachings in my own life. My goal in this book is not to persuade you to shift your faith and abandon Christianity. The teachings of Jesus the Christ are eternal spiritual truths, as I've maintained in previous sections. Jesus is a figure of love and forgiveness, and I do not advocate a dismissal of this wise master teacher. Rather, as you move forward, I believe that your individual relationship with Jesus will greatly improve, if that is what you want. In some denominations, the idol that is Jesus is untouchable, far removed from us humans, or his essence is inaccessible. The psychic ministry reenvisions the identity and role of Jesus, reestablishing the natural and sacred connection you share with this spirit. It openly acknowledges the fundamental truth that there is no separation between you and Jesus, and it demolishes the necessity of an intermediary. It is essential to hold on to eternal truths and maintain your faith in the love and wisdom of God. Know that if it is your will, Jesus will be with you on your journey as well; you will be guided by the light.

Former Christians and many spiritual students in the New Age community have an aversion to the name "Jesus." This very name, and the history of this name, evokes discomfort, suspicion, distrust, and even anger. Many ex-Christians left this particular faith in part because of the symbol of Jesus throughout the ages—which embodies divisiveness, forcible conversion, and condemnation. Spiritual seekers in the New Age / New Thought community intentionally refrain from focusing their attention on Jesus because they either wish to avoid a general association with the historical brutality of Christianity or want to simply acknowledge or embrace the fact that there are multiple routes to God / higher power / all that is—not only through Jesus.

While I am aware of the violence and genocide carried out in the name of Jesus and how this has deeply influenced the general public at large and former

Christians, the psychic path has brought me to the Jesus I did not know before; it has brought to me other spiritual teachers of whom I was unaware for my individual learning and growth. The psychic path has helped me reenvision my identity, and our identity collectively, rebuild my faith, and trust in the *all that is* to truly know that it is given us to know the kingdom of the *all that is* of which we are a part; for the psychic ministry this entails acknowledging that we are, first, spirits and equally divine, and that we are endowed with spiritual gifts. All knowledge is available to everyone, and we are undoubtedly holy creations. Jesus is certainly not a part of everyone's psychic path, and your particular journey will vary on the basis of your own faith and belief system. Nevertheless, you will be guided by those on high who see your holiness and light, and they will guide you forward into your own psychic ministry.

PART II

Reclaiming Your Abilities

Introduction

When I was first learning how to develop to my gifts, I tried various methods, some of which worked beautifully, and others had little to no effect or did not resonate with me. What follows in the next section is simply the end product of various techniques I learned and developed along my path. What I would like to emphasize here is that developing your psychic skills is a process. It simply does not happen overnight. While we live in a society that values instant gratification, be aware that the path of the mystic is a lifelong path. These techniques when practiced accordingly and diligently will help get you there in time.

In the following sections, I have provided a suggested timeline for the development of each ability; of course this is relative to your own development and dependent on what is occurring in your life. My message to you is to never give up, and develop one skill at a time. If you attempt to focus on developing all simultaneously, you will not master any and instead will develop a surface knowledge of each. The goal is to devote your time to each gift and develop them until you feel confident enough to move on to learning the next one.

Meditation is essential as you begin this journey. There are countless books on what meditation is and how to do it. In my own words, meditation allows us to silence the chaotic, egoic mind and tune in to your spirit, the quiet voice within. Meditation is when we choose to actually listen to the guidance of our own inner voice. It is also during this period of silence where we can access preinstalled information and download knowledge from the celestial realms. Meditation also provides an avenue for us to access other realms and communicate with other beings of light and our Higher Self.

In the beginning, it is incredibly important to find a method that aligns with you. There are multiple forms of meditation, and one technique may be more appropriate for you. There are no wrong choices here. When I first started, I was directed to do guided meditations, which worked for me.

Learning how to maintain a focus at the outset is also a significant skill. If we can remove distractions from the mind, we become completely available as useful channels. Most students at the beginning of their journey do not necessarily latch on to the idea of having to sit in silence for thirty minutes with their eyes closed. I know this because I used to be one of them. However, I started off in small segments of time that were manageable, and gradually increased the duration of the meditation period. You can decide whether you want to listen to music as you meditate or you may want to sit in silence. I recommend music that is uplifting and that you feel resonates deeply within your soul. Music is also healing and will assist you to relax as you meditate.

Meditation also enables us to communicate with otherworldly beings. As you practice, you will begin to feel and notice a shift in your abilities, and the messages you receive will become clearer. We are constantly surrounded by a divine, loving support system, which communicates with us often. It is our divine right to communicate with them as they aid us on our journey here on the Earth plane. We must remember that it is really our responsibility to reopen the door to our natural abilities to help each other here on Earth.

Meditation is a critical element of this journey. When you begin, start small. You may choose to meditate for only five minutes a day and then increase it to ten minutes as you learn to maintain your focus. I have found, along the way, that many students do not like to meditate, or if they do, they choose to sit still for five minutes and expect immediate results. Truthfully, there is no magic number of minutes when it comes to meditation. It is case specific. However, I must stress that it is required to develop your abilities. For some, such as myself, the longer and more often I meditate, the more clarity I have. I personally like the art of meditation and have deepened my connection to the spirit world as such. As you move through each section, you will determine how long you will need to meditate for the expansion of your abilities.

CHAPTER 11

The Basics

Grounding

Before you begin any of the following exercises, it is crucial that you take time to ground yourself. What exactly is grounding? This is a process whereby one extends their energy into the Earth. While it may seem counterintuitive to ground when attempting to access your Higher Self, or any other light being, it actually allows you to focus your attention in your body. According to Daniel et al., grounding "is the act of gathering all of your energies—mental, emotional, and physical—and bringing your thoughts and your feelings into calm and harmonious balance in your body."[1] There are many methods by which to ground yourself. You can do this by placing your hands and feet in soil, by hugging a tree, and by eating meat and root vegetables. The following two techniques are useful to ground your energy before your meditations.

TECHNIQUE I: THE ROOT METHOD (SEE FIGURE 3)
Find a comfortable place to sit and turn off all distracting electronic devices.

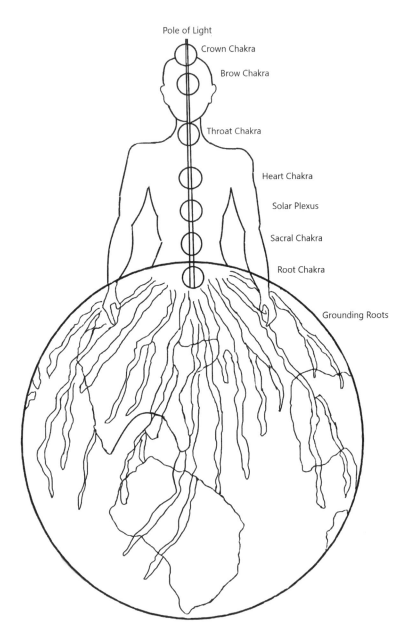

Fig. 3. Grounding energy into the Earth. *Courtesy of Nereida Dominguez.*

Take a series of in-breaths through the nose and exhale through the mouth (repeat ten times).

In your mind's eye, imagine that your feet, ankles, and legs are turning into thick tree roots. Watch them as they penetrate the Earth's soil and expand all the way down into the center of the Earth. You are now grounded.

TECHNIQUE II: HOOK-AND-ANCHOR METHOD
Find a comfortable place to sit and turn off all distracting electronic devices.

Take a series of in-breaths through the nose and exhale through the mouth (repeat ten times).

In your mind's eye, imagine that there is a thick rope chain, with a hook attached to the base of your spine and a large anchor on the other end.

Lower this anchor all the way down to the center of the Earth so that you feel centered and grounded into the Earth. You are now grounded.

Protection
When opening up to the spirit world, it is necessary to protect ourselves from unwanted energies. Before beginning any meditation, you must use a protection technique that resonates with you. In this complex universe, there are forces of energy that are light and dark. As a spiritual force ourself, we encounter all possible living forces. As you open to the spirit realm, you will encounter various types of beings, both light and dark, with varying intentions. While you meditate, you must set your intentions to work only with the highest light. During the early stages of my development, I had a few dark-energy beings present themselves to me as teachers if I so chose to work with them. It is important to be vigilant against these types of energies and protect ourselves. You may keep or remove that shield of protection once your meditation is complete.

Protection Techniques
Golden ball of light: my preferred method. Imagine that you are sitting in a golden ball of light encasing your entire body. See that this ball is reinforced on all sides. You may place your hands on the interior walls of the ball to verify that nothing can penetrate them.

Marshmallow: Imagine in your mind's eye that your body is encased in a thick, white, fluffy marshmallow. Place your hands on the walls of this protective layer to verify that it's reinforced.

Pyramid: In your mind's eye, imagine a three-dimensional glass pyramid of light with a door. Approach the door, open it, and sit in the middle of the floor.

If necessary, you may stand up and place your hands on the glass case to confirm that nothing can penetrate the walls.

Intentionality

It is crucial that you make your intentions known on this journey. Always take note of your own motives. Developing your abilities allows you to be a vessel in which to receive or access information that will be useful and helpful to someone on their life journey. My personal advice would be to sit down and write out all the reasons why you want to develop your abilities, and how you wish to be of service. At the beginning of this journey I knew I wanted to assist people by providing them information that would move them toward some form of healing mentally and emotionally. But truthfully, I was not sure what else I wanted to do with my spiritual abilities. One morning as I sat down to channel a message from the angels, I was confronted about my true intentions. As you open your gifts, there is a level of responsibility to be of service to others in whichever way you choose. After all, you have free will. Always note that even before you speak, your true intentions are always known; therefore, there's no use in pretending. If you intend to use your gifts for personal gain and self-glorification, it will already be known.

Focus

I highly recommend when you start this work that you begin by doing meditations to improve your focus. When I committed to daily practice, I sat for ten to fifteen minutes meditating on a candle flame. While this exercise may initially appear pointless, it will prepare you to properly and effectively develop your abilities. As I was slowly developing, I was unexpectedly visited by a spirit who created a focus exercise for me in which to direct my attention for a set period of time. At the time, I managed to focus my attention for maybe three minutes successfully. Before he departed, he told me that I lacked focus. I made it a point to discipline myself and created the following meditation. I recommend that you practice this meditation daily for many weeks (perhaps two to three or even more) until you have managed to minimize distractions from disrupting your focus.

Focus Meditation

Find a quiet place to sit, and turn off all electronic devices.

Take a series of in-breaths through the nose and exhale through the mouth (Repeat this ten times).

Ground yourself.

Utilize a protective shield to guard your body.

In your mind's eye, imagine that you are sitting at a table with a candle in the center.

Find a lighter or match and light the candle.

Keep your eyes focused on the candle flame for five minutes.

If any thoughts distract you from the flame, simply bring your attention back to your breath and the candle flame.

After successfully completing this meditation, open your eyes.

Repeat this meditation until you can master it for a total of ten minutes.

CHAPTER 12

The Chakra System

Chakras

In this section, I will provide you with a very basic overview of the chakra system; however, I strongly recommend that you read additional literature on this topic to expand your knowledge. So, what are chakras? In Sanskrit, *chakra* means disc or wheel. Chakras are energy centers that exist in the human body.[1] These energy centers run vertically from the base of the spine to the top of the head. There are seven main centers, which include the root, sacral, solar plexus, heart, throat, brow, and crown chakras (see figure 4). According to Anodea Judith, noted author on the chakras, "The content of the chakras is formed largely by repeated patterns from our actions in day-to-day life."[2] These particular patterns are more likely than not acquired from our parents' belief system, which are indoctrinated into our personal belief systems through time. Each chakra develops over a period of seven years, with the root from the ages of 0–7; sacral, 8–15; solar plexus, 16–23; heart, 24–31; brow, 32–39; and crown, 40–47. As one matures from childhood into adulthood, they will develop each chakra, which contain patterns that may be negative, restrictive, or even propitious.[3] Caroline Myss, a spirituality author, maintains that "each chakra represents a spiritual life lesson or challenges common to all human beings."[4] Your chakra system is a critical part of developing your abilities and should be balanced and maintained daily.

The root chakra is located at the base of the spine or between the anus and perineum. It connects and grounds us to the Earth. This energy center encompasses beliefs about survival, security, trust, and your relationship to the material world, as well as the ability for one to provide for himself while here on the Earth plane.[5]

The sacral chakra is located at the sacrum and sexual organs. This chakra encompasses sexuality, pleasure, emotions, nurturance, creative energy, and joy. This chakra affects the appendix, bladder, pelvis, sexual organs, kidneys, reproductive organs, large intestines, and lower vertebrae.[6]

The solar plexus is located a few inches above the navel. This energy center affects the stomach, liver, spleen, pancreas, lower intestines, and gallbladder and regulates the digestive system. Within this chakra resides feelings of fear, as well as your willpower, strength, courage, self-confidence, self-esteem, and even self-respect. This is the seat of your clairsentience.[7]

The heart chakra is located in the center of the chest. This energy center governs the diaphragm, rib cage, lungs, thymus gland, shoulders and arms, and the "circulation of energy throughout the entire body."[8] Stored within this energy center is love, anger, hope, forgiveness, compassion, grief, hatred, and bitterness. The heart chakra is one of the most important chakras and connects the lower and upper chakras. With a completely open heart chakra, one can communicate easily with other light beings. Additionally, if you are struggling to open your crown chakra, you should work on this chakra, since the two are deeply connected.

The throat chakra is located near the larynx and the cervical vertebrae. This chakra is the seat of your clairaudience and enables you to hear. This energy center governs the throat, mouth, teeth and gums, thyroid, esophagus, parathyroid, trachea, neck, jaw, and windpipe. This chakra is the seat of communication, self-expression, speaking our truth, sound, criticism, and telepathy.[9]

The brow or third-eye chakra is located slightly above the center between your eyebrows. This center governs the pineal gland, pituitary gland, brain, eyes, face, and sinuses. The third eye houses clairvoyance and clairgustance. It stores self-knowledge, truth, intellect, open-mindedness, enlightenment, and thought.[10]

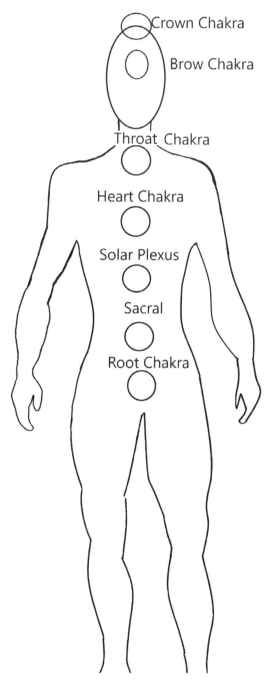

Fig. 4. The chakra system. *Courtesy of Nereida Dominguez.*

The crown chakra, located at the top of the head, is the seventh chakra. This center also governs the pineal gland, the skin, and the muscular and skeletal system.[11] An open crown chakra enables one to channel higher realms.

Why is it important to open, clear, and balance your system for psychic development? The chakras are centers that host psychic information and energy. By opening, clearing, and balancing these centers, we enable the flow of energy, increase the ability to awaken specific centers, and can tune in to our natural abilities. When your chakras are congested with negative thought patterns of fear, anger, doubt, and sadness, then the flow of psychic energy becomes restricted and we experience psychic blocks.

There are countless books that provide various ways to clear your chakras. This is not meant to be an exegesis on chakras, but I am including information here about how I learned to open, clear, and close my chakras.

CLEARING CHAKRAS: FOOD CONSUMPTION
The consumption of specific types of fruits and vegetables will aid in the clearing of your chakras.

Root chakra: red apples, strawberries, cherries, and red root vegetables
Sacral chakra: oranges, cantaloupe, mango, and papaya
Solar plexus: bananas and pineapples
Heart chakra: spinach, green leaf lettuce, and other leafy greens and beets
Throat chakra: water
Brow and crown chakras: It is recommended that a person consider fasting (dependent on your own medical history) to clear these chakras. Consult with your medical physician before attempting this practice.

CLEARING CHAKRAS: THE LORD'S PRAYER
The Lord's Prayer, which can be found in the book of Matthew, has been used to open and clear the chakras during meditation, with each line corresponding as follows:[12]

Crown chakra: Our Father, who art in Heaven
Brow chakra: Hallowed by thy name
Throat chakra: Thy kingdom come
Heart chakra: Thy will be done, on Earth as it is in Heaven
Solar plexus: Give us this day our daily bread
Sacral chakra: Forgive our debts as we forgive our debtors

Root chakra: Lead us not into temptation but deliver us from evil. For thine is the kingdom, the power and the glory forever. Amen.

Visualization techniques are extremely useful for opening and clearing your chakras. You may have to begin visualizing your chakras at the beginning if you do not automatically see anything or feel anything. There is nothing wrong with this. Use whatever form of imagining is easiest for you. Through time as you practice, you will notice a shift in how you see or feel when opening and clearing your chakras. Everyone experiences this process differently. For some, they will begin to see their chakras, their size and color, any blocks or holes, or dark spots that might be present. For others, they will hear the sound of their chakras opening and spinning. Always know that whatever you are experiencing is necessary for your development and growth. For some of us, growth is slow and feels extremely tedious, and yet for others, growth is very fast. Remember: Go your own pace. I am providing a chakra-clearing meditation here, using white light to open and clear the chakras, and a sacred golden toothbrush to cleanse them.

CHAKRA-CLEARING MEDITATION
Find a quiet place to sit, and turn off all electronic devices.
Take a series of in-breaths through the nose and exhale through the mouth (do at least ten of these).
Ground yourself by seeing in your mind's eye your feet, ankles, and legs transform into thick tree roots. Watch them as they penetrate the soil of the Earth. Feel them move through the dirt and expand. As the tips of your roots approach the center of the Earth, you will see a white ball of light resting there. During deep inhales and exhales, your roots enter into this ball of light.
Watch this white ball of light rise up through your roots, moving forward toward your feet, ankles, legs, thighs, and waist.
Allow this light to sit at your waist as you open your red root chakra at the base of your spine. Open this chakra, and watch a red disc spin in the front and back of your body. Imagine a golden toothbrush, and use it to scrub away and cleanse any blemishes and dark spots. Make sure to breathe as it cleanses your chakra. Send white light to this chakra and fill in any noticeable holes. Now watch this white light move up to your sacral chakra.
Open the sacral chakra, located at the area below your naval, and watch an orange disc spin in the front and back of your body. Use the golden toothbrush to scrub away and cleanse any blemishes and dark spots. Make sure to breathe

as it cleanses your chakra. Send white light to this chakra and fill in any noticeable holes. Now watch this white light move up to your solar plexus chakra.

Open the solar plexus chakra, located above your navel, and watch a yellow disc spin in the front and back of your body. Use the golden toothbrush to scrub away and cleanse any blemishes and dark spots. Make sure to breathe as it cleanses your chakra. Send white light to this chakra and fill in any noticeable holes. Now watch this white light move up to your heart chakra.

Open the heart chakra, located in the center of your chest, and watch a green disc spin in the front and back of your body. Use the golden toothbrush to scrub away and cleanse any blemishes and dark spots. Make sure to breathe as it cleanses your chakra. Send white light to this chakra and fill in any noticeable holes. Now watch this white light move up to your throat chakra.

Open the throat chakra, located in the center of your chest, and watch a light-blue disc spin in the front and back of your body. Use the golden toothbrush to scrub away and cleanse any blemishes and dark spots. Make sure to breathe as it cleanses your chakra. Send white light to this chakra and fill in any holes. Now watch this white light move up to your brow chakra.

Open the brow chakra, located above the center of the eyebrows, and watch an indigo disc spin in the front and back of your head. Use the golden toothbrush to scrub away and cleanse any blemishes and dark spots. Make sure to breathe as it cleanses your chakra. Send white light to this chakra and fill in any noticeable holes. Now watch this white light move up to your crown chakra.

Open the crown chakra, located at the crown of the head, and watch a violet disc spin. Use the golden toothbrush to scrub away and cleanse any blemishes and dark spots. Make sure to breathe as it cleanses your chakra. Send white light to this chakra and fill in any noticeable holes in this chakra. Now watch this white light erupt out of your crown chakra and encase the body in pure white light. Take five deep breaths in and exhale out of the mouth. Open your eyes.

CHAPTER 13

The Clairs

Clairvoyance: Opening Your Third Eye

At the introductory stages of psychic development, many people want to develop clairvoyance and open their third eye—and understandably so. Clairvoyance, which is defined as clear seeing, enables us to see behind the veil of this world. This includes the ability to see angels, guides, elementals, archangels, and even deceased loved ones. Your third eye is the gateway to your inner sight to seeing other realms and light beings. Your clairvoyance sits in your third-eye chakra, which must be consistently exercised like a physical muscle for its growth. Thus, it is necessary to spend time strengthening this chakra. However, the chakra system works cohesively, and one chakra cannot fully grow and function while the others are insufficiently balanced. Therefore, it is crucial to continually cleanse and balance your chakras on a daily basis.

It may take several months to a year to open your third eye. The development of your abilities is dependent on your own growth. As students of this universe, we each have a very specialized curriculum designed to help us grow and progress at a rate that is beneficial for us. Do not get frustrated, do not compare your journey to someone else's, and do not give up.

How do you know that your third eye is opening? During the initial stages of meditation, you will begin by seeing a variety of colors. Upon further practice, these colors will shift into sparks of light. These sparks are telltale signs that your eye is opening. These sparks are actually your spirit guides, archangels, and guardian angels that surround you on a daily basis. The more you meditate, the more you will see them. As your consciousness expands through meditative practice, you may begin to see colorful orbs around you as well. Do not be alarmed, since all these are to be expected. In addition, you will feel pulsing sensations in your third eye or throbbing in your brow chakra. I suggest that to develop this clair, practice the given meditations at least once a day for many months. This may appear to be an insurmountable mountain to climb, but know that your efforts are not in vain.

I have found that many people assume once their clairvoyance is developed, they will be able to see light beings with the naked eye in full form. And for some, this does occur, but for most, it does not. We may see these beings as we expect to see them in meditation, but they also may present themselves as sparks of light, big flashes of white and gold light, and colorful orbs.

Clairvoyance also provides us the gift of seeing possible future events for ourselves and others. Some clairvoyants may see a complete event occurring in a linear format, while others may receive only pieces of a puzzle that they will have to assemble over a period of time. As on Earth, the universe speaks to us in various languages. At times, we will receive a message through symbols, such as animals, numbers, and universally understood religious symbology. Be aware that your guide and angels will choose a language that resonates with you, and it is up to you to decipher those messages. I personally recommend creating your own symbolic dictionary.

In meditation, your spiritual support team will provide you with many different symbols to answer your questions. Utilize a journal to document each symbol and what that symbol means for you. Given that many symbols are co-opted by various cultures and then redefined/reinterpreted, it is up to you to define it for yourself. You may choose to look up the symbol online or even in a book and then write the definition in your dictionary. Your guides and angels will know your personal interpretation of your symbols and will reference them as such to answer your future questions.

Awakening the Psychic Self

MEDITATION: THE DOOR METHOD

Find a quiet place to sit, and turn off all electronic devices.
Take a series of in-breaths through the nose and exhale through the mouth (do at least ten of these).

First, do a brief chakra-clearing exercise. Do one of your own choosing, or you may do the one I have placed here in this book.

Ground yourself by seeing in your mind's eye your feet, ankles, and legs transforming into thick tree roots. Watch them as they penetrate the soil of the Earth. Feel them move through the dirt and expand. As the tips of your roots approach the center of the Earth, you will begin to see a golden ball of light. As you breathe, your roots enter this ball of light.

Imagine this golden light traveling up your roots and into your feet and ankles, progressing up your legs, and then reaching your waist, climbing up your chest, reaching your neck and shoulders, extending down your arms, and then traveling all the way to your hands.

Imagine this light now climbing up your back and your neck and encasing your entire head. Your whole body is now completely gold.

Use a protective method suitable for you, and place this around your body.

Bring your attention to your mind's eye, and imagine that you are standing in the middle of a long hallway with a door at the end. Begin to walk to the door.

Invite your guide, your angels, or both to be with you during this time, and thank them for their presence.

As you approach this door, look at it to see if there's anything unique about the door and the door handle.

Think of a question that you would like answered, and on the count of three, push the door open and walk through.

You may see a symbol of some sort, a color, or a number. Know that this is your answer. Make note of this symbol, turn around, leave, and close the door behind you.

Take a deep breath in through the nose, and exhale out the mouth. Open your eyes and make sure to document your messages and symbols.

Note that the more you practice this meditation, the images and messages will become clearer and stronger.

MEDITATION: GOLDEN BALL OF LIGHT

Find a quiet place to sit, and turn off all electronic devices.

Take a series of in-breaths through the nose and exhale through the mouth (do at least ten of these).

First, do a brief chakra-clearing exercise. Do one of your own choosing, or you may do the one I have placed here in this book.

Ground yourself by seeing in your mind's eye your feet, ankles, and legs transforming into thick tree roots. Watch them as they penetrate the soil of the Earth. Feel them move through the dirt and expand. As the tips of your roots approach the center of the Earth, you will begin to see a golden ball of light. As you breathe, your roots enter into this ball of light.

Imagine this golden light traveling up your roots and into your feet and ankles and up your legs, and then reaching your waist, climbing up your chest, reaching your neck and shoulders, and extending down your arms and all the way to your hands.

Imagine this light now climbing up your back and your neck and encasing your entire head. Your whole body is now completely gold.

Imagine that a golden ball of light is moving down the center of your head into your third eye. See this bright golden ball of light begin to spin in your third eye. As it rotates, it becomes brighter and brighter until it expands across your forehead.

At this point, I want you to invite your guides and angels to be present with you.

Ask a question of your choosing and focus your mind gently on this golden light.

Watch for any symbols or messages. You may open your eyes and document your messages.

Please note that this meditation also works to clear your third eye.

MEDITATION: THE GOLDEN ELEVATOR

Find a quiet place to sit, and turn off all electronic devices.

First, do a brief chakra-clearing exercise. Do one of your own choosing, or you may do the one I have placed here in this book.

Ground yourself by seeing in your mind's eye your feet, ankles, and legs transforming into thick tree roots. Watch them as they penetrate the soil of the Earth. Feel them move through the dirt and expand. As the tips of your roots approach the center of the Earth, you will begin to see a golden ball of light. As you breathe, your roots enter into this ball of light.

Imagine this golden light traveling up your roots and into your feet and ankles and up your legs, and then reaching your waist, climbing up your chest, reaching your neck and shoulders, extending down your arms and all the way to your hands.

Imagine this light now climbing up your back and your neck and encasing your entire head. Your whole body is now completely gold.

Use a protective method suitable for you, and place this around your body.

Invite your angels and your guides of the highest light to be present. Ask them a question to be answered in meditation.

In your mind's eye, I want you to imagine that you are standing in front of an elevator with two golden doors. Push the button to open the doors. Walk into the elevator and look for the button numbered "30." As the doors close, you begin to feel yourself go up the first floor, the second, the third, etc. Watch the buttons light up as you move up closer to the thirtieth floor.

Once you reach the thirtieth floor the doors will open. As you walk forward you will see a golden pathway open up before you. Walk down this path and look to the right; you will see a box or a chest. Open it and take the gift that's inside. This gift is the answer to your question. Return to the elevator and descend down to the first floor. The doors will open and you will walk out. Take a deep breath, state your name aloud three times, and open your eyes. Document the answer to your question.

Developing Clairaudience

Clairaudience is a French word that means clear hearing. This specifically involves hearing beyond the limitations of our senses. The throat chakra is the seat of your clairaudience. A blocked throat chakra is a major challenge to developing clairaudience. If you have trouble speaking up and standing your ground or are unable to communicate your thoughts clearly, you likely have a blocked throat chakra. A clairaudient individual may indeed be able to attune themselves to hear the voices of departed loved ones, Earthbound spirits, angels, and guides. As I learned throughout my journey, clairaudience requires the ability to discern between the spirits. Unbeknown to many people, there are many types of spirits that surround us daily, some of which attempt to interact with us directly, and others are merely coexisting. Regardless, it is our responsibility to learn how to differentiate between them as we become attuned to hearing the spirit world. There are two ways that you will hear the voice of a spirit: in your inner ear or outer ear. Messages that are given in your inner ear are done so through telepathy. At times, this voice will sound as if it is your own. However, the message itself will be unique and in opposition to your natural tone and speech. If you possess the gift of external hearing, then you will hear voices speak to you as if they are in the same room. These voices will at times sound like a whisper or a full-fledged human voice completely different from your own. As your hearing develops, you may experience the following symptoms:

A. A pulsing sensation in the ear that is opening. Our hearing develops one ear at a time. You may feel a throbbing sensation, or more commonly you may continually feel and hear puffs of air in your ear. These are common phenomena and can last for many months as you focus on developing your clairaudience. These sensations may occur consistently throughout the day or periodically throughout the month. Clairaudience can be a challenging ability to develop. However, with daily committed practice, it can be done. So how does one develop their hearing? First, set your intention. Announce to your guide that you are ready to begin working on this ability. And make sure that you devote an adequate amount of time to practice. Meditation is required as always.

B. Opening and clearing the throat chakra: It is necessary to do a chakra-clearing meditation that works for you. I am offering one here, but there are many that are available. Clear and balance all the chakras; however, when you reach the throat chakra, ensure that you expand this chakra more than the rest. You can imagine in your mind's eye that your ears are literally growing and expanding in size beyond your whole body. You may also want to send golden light to your ears, and imagine that this light is cleaning your ears from the inside out.

C. Listen to music: Listen to a long piece of classical music containing an orchestra, and pay close attention to one instrument throughout the entire orchestra. This will assist you with fine tuning your hearing and enable you to clearly hear through the celestial "white noise."

D. Sing! Singing is one of the best ways to develop your clairaudience. Sing aloud every day.

E. Chanting: Chanting will further increase your ability to hear spirit. There are many different types of chants—find one that resonates with you and practice daily.

F. Play music: If you are a musician, chances are that your spiritual hearing is probably already well developed and needs only fine tuning. If not, then learn to play an instrument or even see live music shows. You do not have to become proficient or a virtuoso.

All of these will help you to hear the spirit world. Many people wonder how long they should practice. I personally recommend that you commit to at least three to six months of daily practice. Of course, this is all relative to your own development, but for budding psychics, I strongly advise that you commit to a schedule of practice. You will know when this ability is developing as you begin to hear whispers and other dissonant voices, some of which will whisper your name repeatedly until your hearing expands.

Developing Clairsentience

"Clairsentience" simply means clear feeling or clear sensing. Every person experiences a wide range of emotions daily; however, many of us fail to notice that in addition to our own feelings, we are absorbing and sensing the emotions of those we are in contact with throughout the day. A person who is clairsentient can feel the presence of otherworldly beings and the emotions of others and detect multiple forms of energy. Most of us can tell when something does not feel right. Unbeknown to us, we are actually using our natural ability, our clairsentience, to digest and assess a situation.

Your clairsentience is housed in your solar plexus. It is essential to clear and balance this chakra to develop your clairsentience. Again, while it is important to focus on this chakra, do not fail to balance the entire system.

When surrounded by negative people, we have a tendency to feel and, at times, absorb their sadness, anxiety, and frustration, and we internalize those forms of energy. The same occurs when we encounter people who are upbeat, happy, joyful, optimistic, and positive; we suddenly feel joyous, uplifted, and optimistic ourselves. We are subtly reading and accessing that form of energy.

As I stated earlier, many light beings coexist alongside us without our knowledge. There are some of us who may sense that someone or something else is in the room with us, but can't see it or hear it. It is your clairsentience that alerts you. How does one fine-tune their clairsentience to sense/feel the presence of other energies?

A. Meditate daily. Meditation is essential for the development of all abilities.

B. Set your intention: Decide if you want to practice developing your clairsentience with your guide or your guardian angels, and tell them. Make your intentions clear at the start.

Sensing Energy

Learn to sense the energy of your guide: Find a quiet place to sit, set up protection, and ground yourself. Complete the chakra-clearing meditation. Call in your spirit guide verbally: Make sure you state that you choose to work only with the guide who is aligned with your higher holy self. Ask him or her to stand to your right and then your left. Practice detecting the subtle changes of energy—you may feel a sudden wave of dizziness, a cloud of pressure above your head, a wave of cool air, or a sudden cool breeze, and you may even feel lighter. All of these signify the presence of a spirit being. There is no wrong answer here. I have read in many works by well-known practitioners that "cool air" is an indicator of a negative presence; however, this was not my experience, and my angels have presented themselves to me with big breezes of cool air, which followed the flapping of their wings.

Call in your guardian angels and repeat step 1. Notice if you smell flowers or even fruit, which is a telltale sign that they are with you.

Journal it! Notice the subtle differences between both types of energy.

Practice this daily. The more you practice, the more familiar their energy will be, and you will acquire greater discernment.

THE FLOWER METHOD

When you are in the beginning stages of developing your clairsentience, you will want to be able to detect all types of energy. In this exercise, you will practice detecting the different types of energy among a variety of flowers.

First, do a brief chakra-clearing exercise. Do one of your own choosing, or you may do the one I have placed here in this book.

Ground yourself by seeing in your mind's eye your feet, ankles, and legs transforming into thick tree roots. Watch them as they penetrate the soil of the Earth. Feel them move through the dirt and expand. As the tips of your roots approach the center of the Earth, you will begin to see a golden ball of light. As you breathe, your roots enter into this ball of light.

Imagine this golden light traveling up your roots and into your feet and ankles and up your legs and then reaching your waist, climbing up your chest, reaching your neck and shoulders, extending down your arms and all the way to your hands.

Imagine this light now climbing up your back and your neck and encasing your entire head. Your whole body is now completely gold.

Use a protective method suitable for you and place this around your body.

Find at least five different flowers.

Open hand chakras: Rub your hands together for thirty seconds.

Pick one flower and place it in the palm of one hand and cover it with the other hand. Close your eyes and concentrate on "feeling the energy" of that flower. The energy may take a short while for you to feel it. You may feel a throbbing sensation in your hands, subtle waves of vibrations, or even as if the flower is pulsating. Notice if the energy is strong or light. Journal it.

Repeat steps 7 and 8 with the remaining flowers. This exercise can also be completed by using a variety of crystals. I personally recommend when you are trying to develop this ability that you practice daily for at least five weeks to see major progress. Do not feel defeated, and know that everyone feels/senses energy differently.

Raising Your Vibration

As you begin to shift your consciousness into the realm of the metaphysical, you will encounter a lot of literature encouraging you to "raise your vibration" in order to be able to see, hear, and even feel spirit. What does this mean, exactly? Every living thing contains consciousness, and its life force energetically vibrates at a very specific rate. This goes for your spirit, angels, archangels, elementals, spirit guides, and other beings as well. Given that we are existing on the Earth plane, we vibrate at a very dense rate as opposed to "otherworldly" beings. In order for us to communicate with other light beings, it is necessary to raise our vibration to hear, see, and feel beyond the five Earthly senses. How is this accomplished?

Rest: The mind and body need sufficient rest to raise your vibration. Any form of energy work can be physically exhausting and deplete our energy storehouse; therefore, we must rest to be rejuvenated and replenish our energy.

Diet and exercise: A balanced diet is crucial in order to communicate with spirit. Everything in moderation. I was personally advised to minimize my sugar intake, since this would "clog" my channel. The angels encourage the consumption of water and a healthy dose of fruits and vegetables throughout the day. Exercise is about maintaining a healthy body and a clear channel to receive information from the divine source. Our body is the vessel we use to help us communicate; therefore, we must take care of it and respect its mission as well.

Positivity and optimism: Maintaining a positive and optimistic attitude is an essential ingredient in elevating one's vibration. The energy of positivity vibrates at a very high level, thus elevating our ability to connect to lighter and powerful spirits. The same goes with optimism. Approach each situation, regardless of how bleak it may appear on the surface, with complete optimism. Know that you are always helped and never alone. Pessimism and negativity lower your vibration and prevent you from being able to have a strong connection. Also, maintain an attitude of gratitude.

Laughter: Laughing is a great way to lift one's energy and vibration. At times, when people are laughing, they get the sensation that they are floating on air—this is how it feels when we are raising our vibration.

Nature: Go out into nature. Connect with the healing and loving energy of Mother Earth. Go for a long walk along the beach or in the woods or meditate near a tree or in a field of flowers. This will instantly lift your vibration.

CHAPTER 14

Connecting with Spirit Guides and Angels

Your spirit guide is an advanced being of light that has previously incarnated into human form. Guides have lived many lifetimes on this planet to grow their soul, as we are doing now. Guides are not your deceased loved ones. They are beings of light that you chose to help you throughout your journey on planet Earth until your transition. Guides act as your support system and are helping you through your selected life lessons. You may have known them from previous lifetimes or not at all. You have chosen them because they have mastered the lessons you wish to learn and would be the best guide to help you here on Earth. You actually have many guides who come in and out of your life to assist you with specific lessons or events, especially when you are learning a new skill or navigating a new challenge. With that said, there is one main guide that is always there to help and guide you. That particular guide has been with you since your incarnation and will be with you until your transition back to the spirit world. So, how do you work with them?

Acknowledge them: State aloud that you are aware of their presence. Tell them you would like to establish a relationship with them and work with them.

Get your guide's name: The following technique comes from spiritual teacher and author Sonia Choquette.[1]

You may ask for their name out loud, or silently within the mind, in the evening or morning while lying down in bed. Wait patiently for an answer. Please note that this may take several weeks to accomplish. Do not get frustrated and do not give up.

Verification: Once you hear a name (and please know that they likely will have an "average" name such as Jennifer, Casey, or even Isabel), ask for verification. You can do this by giving them a few symbols you would like them to present to you within a few weeks' time. An example could be a hawk, a blue feather, or a rainbow. Our guides may show us these symbols on a T-shirt, on a TV show, or even on a card. These symbols confirm that you heard their name correctly and they indeed are your guide. Pay attention—it is your job!

Ask your guide to meet you in your dreams: Before going to bed at night, ask your guide to present himself or herself in the dream world, and trust that they will.

Meditation: More likely than not, you will meet your guide in a meditative state. There is a meditation included here to help you meet and interact with your guide. Know that they present themselves when they feel you are ready.

Tarot cards: If Tarot resonates with you, I advise you to interact with your guide through this symbolic system. Clear and shuffle your cards and ask your guide for a card that is representative of him/her and pull one card. From that card you will have gained insight into your guide and his/her personality.

Pendulum: Communication with your guide can also be done by using a pendulum, which is another divination tool that enables us to communicate with spirit. You can purchase one online or in a metaphysical store. After clearing your pendulum with sage, you can set the intention to work only with your guide who is in alignment with your higher self. From there, you may use it to communicate. (Ask it to show you yes and no. Note the direction it moves for each response. Ask it if it is in alignment with your higher self. If the answer is no, then you will have to clear it and ask again. If the answer is yes, then proceed with communicating.)

Music: An additional fun way to communicate with your guide is through music. Ask your guide at night before you fall asleep to please give you a message for the next day through a song. When you wake up, know that a song will be playing. Look up the lyrics of the portion of the song that is playing to find your message.

SPIRIT GUIDE MEDITATION
Find a quiet place to sit, and turn off all electronic devices.

Take a series of in-breaths through the nose and exhale through the mouth (do at least ten of these).

Ground yourself by seeing in your mind's eye your feet, ankles, and legs transforming into thick tree roots. Watch them as they penetrate the soil of the Earth. Feel them move through the dirt and expand. As the tips of your roots approach the center of the Earth, you will begin to see a white ball of light. As you breathe, watch your roots enter into this ball of light.

Watch this white ball of light rise up through your roots, moving forward toward your feet, ankles, legs, thighs, waist, torso, and shoulders and then down your arms and hands. This light now climbs up your neck and face and encases your entire head and body.

Utilize a protective shield to cover your body.

Open your chakras.

See within your mind's eye an enormous tree. Walk to this tree and ask your spirit guide of the highest light to meet with you. You are going to climb to the top of this tree until you reach a landing. Count to fifty as you climb.

Once you reach the landing, a rainbow pathway will unfold before you. Walk down this path toward a house. Once you reach this house, look for a key to open the door.

Walk into this house and look around. Familiarize yourself with the style of the furniture and the decor. Notice if it's reminiscent of any particular time period. You are going to climb the stairs of this house and choose a door to any of the rooms. Look at the door to see if anything is written on it. Notice if it is a particular color or style.

Walk through the door and you will see two empty chairs in the room. Sit in one chair and ask your spirit guide to come in the room and sit in the chair beside you.

Once he/she appears, ask them if they are aligned with your higher holy self. If they say no, ask them to leave, and ask for a new guide. If this guide says yes, then they can stay.

You may ask them any questions you like. Once you are through, thank them for being there, and then leave the house. Walk down the rainbow path and climb down the tree, and make sure to count down from fifty to one. Once you reach the bottom, say your name out loud three times, and then open your eyes.

How to Work with Angels and Archangels

As we incarnate into the Earth plane, we are assigned at least two guardian angels to help us during our journey. We are told in the Bible that God has provided us with angels to guard us.[2] They do serve as protectors, but they also operate as guides, helpers, and comforters. They are gentle, loving beings who have never incarnated into physical form. Angels communicate with us much like guides do. However, they definitely work with us by providing messages through numbers and other symbols. Most people are familiar with angel numbers. If you personally haven't experienced this phenomenon but would like to, ask your guardian angels to work with you in this format. It is important to pay attention to recurring numbers that cross your path. I recommend Doreen Virtue's book *Angel Numbers* to understand the message.[3] You may also work with your angels the same way you do with your guide. You may engage with them through meditation, a pendulum, music, and dreams.

Another way of working with your angels is by utilizing angel oracle decks. While we are still in the early stages of development and have not quite opened our clairaudience or clairvoyance, this tool can be useful in communicating with your angels. And even when you have fully developed, they are great tools to consult your angels for answers! On a personal note, I do believe in the power of prayer and suggest a prayer over your deck each time it is used to guarantee an answer that is in alignment with your higher holy self and for your highest good.

Additionally, you may choose to call on and work with the archangels whenever you choose. Most of us are familiar with the archangels listed in the Bible—Michael and Gabriel. Like the angels, archangels have never incarnated into human form; they are a separate species. Each archangel is assigned a different role by which to aid you here. In many texts, you will find that there exists a Heavenly "hierarchy" of angelic beings organized into three spheres, which include the following orders: Principalities, Powers, Virtues, Dominions, Thrones, Cherubim, Seraphim, archangels, and angels.

The First Sphere: Surround the Throne of God
Seraphim: "The Burning or Fiery Ones." The order closest to God. They constantly sing and praise God.
Cherubim: "Fullness of Wisdom." Also known as guardians of the stars and the light.
Thrones: "Many-Eyed Ones." The order responsible for divine justice and judicial power.

The Second Sphere: Responsible for Heavenly Order[4]
Dominions: Govern the lesser angels.
Powers: Maintain the balance of the universe. They are also the angels of birth and death.
Virtues: Govern Heavenly bodies. Execute orders of the dominions. Responsible for working miracles on Earth.

The Third Sphere: Messenger Angels[5]
Principalities: "Protectors of Religion." Responsible for watching over leaders and rulers of people and nations.
Archangels: Celestial messenger angels.
Angels: Closest to humans. Holy messengers. Traditionally recognized as guardian angels.

The most commonly known archangels are Michael, Raphael, Gabriel, and Uriel. However, many others are mentioned in the Scrolls of Qumran and in the Book of Enoch.[6] While these angels are commonly known as archangels, they operate within different spheres of the celestial order.

Here are some of the most acknowledged archangels and their roles:[7]

Ariel: His name means "Lion or Lioness of God." Angel of courage.
Azrael: Angel of Death. His name means "Whom God helps." Order of the Archangels.
Chamuel: His name means "He who seeks or sees God." Order of Cherubim.

Gabriel: Angel of wisdom, mercy, and revelation. He is commonly recognized as the messenger angel in the Bible. In Hebrew, Gabriel means "the Mighty One" and "Hero of God." His name also means "God is my strength." Order of the Cherubim.
Haniel: His name means "Glory of God." Order of the Principalities.
Jeremiel or Remiel: His name means "Mercy of God."
Jophiel: Angel of beauty. Her name means "Beauty of God." Jophiel is also known to assist artists and creative projects. Order of the Cherubim.
Metatron: His name means "Angel of the Presence." Order of the Seraphim.
Michael: Angel of protection. His name means "He who is like God." Order of the Seraphim.
Raguel: His name means "Friend of God."
Raphael: Angel of Healing. His name means "God heals." Order of the Cherubim.
Raziel: His name means "Secret of God."
Sandalphon: His name means "Brother" in Greek.
Uriel: Angel of light and fire. His name means "God is my light" or "Fire of God." Order of the Cherubim.
Zadkiel or Hesediel: Angel of freedom and Mercy. In Hebrew his name means "Righteousness of God." Order of Dominions.

Although I have attributed a specific gender to each archangel, please note that in truth, they are genderless but may present themselves to you as either gender. There are many books that provide various techniques by which to invoke the archangels. Truthfully, it is just as simple to say, "I invoke archangel _____," and they will appear. Angels and archangels are omnipresent and can be everywhere at once. The angels and archangels do not judge if your problem is big or small; they simply want to help you whenever they can. I have provided a meditation to assist you with working with the archangels and your guardian angels.

ANGEL AND ARCHANGEL MEDITATION: STAIRCASE TO HEAVEN
Find a quiet place to sit, and turn off all electronic devices.

Take a series of in-breaths through the nose and exhale through the mouth (do at least ten of these).
Ground yourself by seeing in your mind's eye your feet, ankles, and legs transform into thick tree roots. Watch them as they penetrate the soil of the Earth. Feel them move through the dirt and expand. As the tips of your roots approach the center of the Earth, you will begin to see a white ball of light. As you breathe, watch your roots enter this ball of light.

Watch this white light rise up through your roots, moving forward toward your feet, ankles, legs, thighs, and waist. Allow this light to travel up your torso and shoulders, then down your arms and hands. This light will move up your neck and face and encase your entire head and body.

Utilize a protective shield of your choosing.

Open and cleanse your chakras with white light.

Imagine a long, thin pole running from the crown of your head down through the center of your body, down to your root chakra, all the way down to the center of the Earth.

See liquid white light poured into the top of the pole, and watch it flow down your pole all the way down to the center of the Earth.

Imagine in your mind's eye a long and winding staircase that reaches above the clouds and to the gates of Heaven.

Climb this staircase and count to fifty. At the top, you will see a set of pearly white gates. On the other side of these gates is a shimmery white path. Move beyond the gates and walk this path. In your mind, ask for your guardian angel or a specific archangel to be present. As you walk this path, you will see a small garden with a water fountain and bench in the distance. Sit down on this bench, and ask your angel to meet you there.

An angel will walk toward you and sit on the bench next to you. Ask him/her any questions you desire.

Once you are finished, thank your angel and return to the gates and climb back down the staircase. Make sure to count down from fifty to one. Once you reach the bottom, take a series of in-breaths and exhale. Say your name three times out loud and open your eyes.

Prayer

Many people who are navigating a new spiritual path question the role that prayer plays in the development of their spirituality. As you shift away from a consciousness that is bound by very strict rules and regulations, you will begin to question what to keep and what to leave behind. While prayer has been eschewed in some New Age communities, I have learned how important this communication is for our development and soul growth. As spirits, we exist in the mind of the creator. Our spirits are connected to the *all that is*, the God source, eternally, and thus we naturally have an open channel in which to communicate.

Prayer is the medium of communication between that which is source (creator, God) and that which is spirit (created). Although most understand prayer to be a mode of supplication and petition for something or someone, prayer is actually a medium through which we commune with the creator spirit. Every one of us is a channel for the divine, since the channel has been preinstalled and is our right as divine children of the *all that is*. We may choose to ignore this fact, but it does not negate it.

Those who are transitioning from a hierarchal system of consciousness, or religion and doctrine, might choose to abandon this component of their practice. As stated earlier, many people have become dispirited by the idea of having to pray to a "judgmental" entity for assistance (traditionally envisioned as a male figure). Implicit in this is the belief that we are separated and thus "lower" or "inferior" to our creator. This is indeed not so. All are one. This belief in duality, high/low, up/down, and superior/inferior is a manmade concept that does not serve us here and has no room in prayer, or in our relationship with the creator spirit. It is important for those who are struggling with their understanding of prayer to reenvision its intended purpose.

Through a committed practice of meaningful prayers focused on love, forgiveness, and gratitude, we purify and enhance our channels, which gives way to stronger psychic abilities. How does this work? When we perform "psychic" work, the heart is one of the most valuable tools and must be open to bridge the worlds for communication. Prayer opens the heart chakra through a process of purification. Purification occurs during our moments with God when our hearts have the courage to open and confess our true fears, our mistakes, or our inability to forgive or let go of the past. In these moments, we undress our shadow self and bring our darkness to the light for purification of the heart. This process strengthens our connection with our father-mother, the one, the creator force, the *all that is* in front of him. We become naked to become cleansed. This cleansing process enhances our gifts and connection by removing blocks to love, allowing us to be clear channels to give and receive.

Prayer facilitates alchemy of the mind. Alchemy is the process of transmuting base metals into gold or, in this case, transmuting fear-based thinking into love-based thinking. The mind, when obstructed and fear based, can be a death sentence, but a purified mind when joined with a purified heart can be utilized to heal the world. Psychic work cannot be performed with a closed heart and fearful mind. Prayer enables alchemy to occur once we have brought our hearts and minds to be cleansed, healed, and christened, or transformed into gold.

CHAPTER 15

Tools and Exercises for Psychic Expansion

Expanding the Mind: The Diamond Exercise

While I was teaching my first advanced clairvoyance class, I was instructed by my guide to teach students a new method to expand their abilities. This exercise involves using the healing properties of a three-dimensional white diamond to expand one's clairvoyance and clairaudience (see figure 5). As explained by my guides, the white light of the diamond has a healing and purifying effect. Specifically, it helps to clear the mind and heart to create a clearer channel. Your psychic abilities are thus stronger when your channel is wholly clear. You can practice this meditation as often as you like.

MEDITATION

Find a quiet place to sit, and turn off all electronic devices.

Take a series of deep inhalations through the nose and exhale through the mouth (repeat ten times).

First, perform a brief chakra-clearing exercise. Do one of your own choosing, or you may do the one I have placed here in this book.

Ground yourself by seeing in your mind's eye your feet, ankles, and legs transforming into thick tree roots. Watch them as they penetrate the soil of the Earth. Feel them move through the dirt and expand. As the tips of your roots approach the center of the Earth, you will begin to see a white ball of light. As you breathe, watch your roots enter this ball of light.

Imagine this white light traveling up your roots, into your feet and ankles, and up your legs, and then reaching your waist, climbing up your chest, reaching your neck and shoulders, and extending down your arms and all the way to your hands.

Imagine this light now climbing up your back and your neck and encasing your entire head. Your whole body is now completely white.

Use a protective method suitable for you, and place this around your body.

In your mind's eye, imagine a bright, white, three-dimensional diamond and watch it spin clockwise. See white light emanate from this diamond. As you watch it spin clockwise, relax your mind.

Breathe deeply through the mouth and open your eyes.

THE PYRAMID GROUP EXERCISE: EXPANDING YOUR GIFTS

As explained in the first part of this book, the pyramid is a symbol that has been utilized by many civilizations through time. In a metaphysical sense, this geometric shape embodies the Holy Trinity, that being the Father, the Son, and the Holy Spirit (see figure 6). While the language used here is Christian in nature and may offend some, please note the definitions presented here: the Father—the

Fig. 5. Three-dimensional diamond.

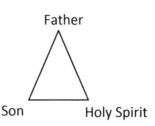

Fig. 6. Group pyramid exercise.

Fig. 7. Three-dimensional diamond.

creator, the all that is; the Son—all spirits, including you, all cocreators; Holy Spirit—the voice for God, the creator voice.

Each side is representative of one part comprising the "Trinity of being," or mind, body, and spirit, or Father, Son, and Holy Spirit.[1] The pyramid itself, as explained by the divine, enables the following to transpire: expansion of gifts/abilities by increasing energy times 3.

This exercise is to be performed by three people with similar energy for it to have the desired effect. As you choose the people you want to work with, you will naturally know where to take your place within the pyramid.

MEDITATION STEPS

As you sit in the pyramid, each person must hold hands to create the shape.
Place a protective shield around your body.
Each person is to visualize in their mind's eye a large three-dimensional diamond (see figure 7).

This diamond will spin clockwise in each person's vision.
Allow the body to relax. Maintain your focus for at least ten minutes. You can practice this as often as you like.

Each person will notice an enhancement in their abilities within one to two weeks.

Mirror Magic: Exploring Your True Self

Mirrors are psychic divination tools that strengthen one's clairvoyance. Through many centuries, mirrors have been used as scrying tools to see past and future events.[2] Some say that mirrors are portals that enable one to walk into other existing realms for answers.[3] They also allow you to tune in to your true self. In my clairvoyance classes, I have been asked by my guide to teach others to use this tool to help them see their true self. As you stand in front of the mirror, it will reflect back the current state of your energy field. It will reflect your light field and any holes, dark spots, blocks, and disturbances in your aura. To heal this, you will be taken to a point in time, or situation in your own life, that is still impeding your growth, or a lesson that you are in the process of learning. It will show you if you are in need of forgiveness, healing, or even a change of perception. I am including here a helpful meditation that will guide you to working with mirrors in meditation. There are many books on using mirrors as scrying tools, since they have a long historical use. However, the intent here is to help you confront inner problems and help you spiritually grow. This meditation may be performed in front of an actual mirror, although it is not necessary.

MIRROR MAGIC MEDITATION

Find a quiet place to sit, and turn off all electronic devices to avoid unnecessary distractions.

Take a series of ten inhalations through the nose and exhale through the mouth.

First, do a brief chakra-clearing exercise. Do one of your own choosing, or you may do the one I have placed here in this book.

Ground yourself by seeing in your mind's eye your feet, ankles, and legs transforming into thick tree roots. Watch them as they penetrate the soil of the Earth. Feel them move through the dirt and expand. As the tips of your roots approach the center of the Earth, you will begin to see a golden ball of light. As you breathe, watch your roots enter this ball of light.

Imagine this golden light traveling up your roots, into your feet and ankles, and up your legs, and then reaching your waist, climbing up your chest, reaching your neck and shoulders, and extending down your arms and all the way to your hands.

Imagine this light now climbing up your back and your neck and encasing your entire head. Your whole body is now completely gold.

Use a protective method suitable for you, and place this around your body.

Bring your attention to your third eye. In your mind's eye, imagine that you are walking down a long hallway toward a set of double doors.

As you approach the doors, place your hands on the doors. Examine its material composition and rub your hands across the door.

Ask your guides and angels to assist you in making this journey to your true self.

On the count of three, place your hands on the door handle and walk through the doors.

You will walk toward a very long and tall mirror. Stand in front of this mirror and ask out loud: Show me my true self.

Trust that you are seeing what is necessary for your own growth and consciousness.

Ask the following questions: (a) Where are my blocks? (b) Where are my imbalances? (c) What are my strengths? (d) What should I begin to heal?

Once you have completed your experience, return from where you came and take a series of deep breaths in through the nose and then exhale through the mouth. Open your eyes and document your findings.

Online Courses

Within the past ten years, there has been an explosion of online psychic-development classes. These range from opening your third eye to meeting spirit guides to chakra healing, mediumship, and many more. Psychic practitioners offer their classes online hoping to reach a broader audience and make training more accessible. They also have the opportunity to collaborate with other practitioners to develop stronger training modules for students. The internet has become a useful platform for teachers to aid in the facilitation of a global awakening.

For the most part I am an advocate of this medium of learning and training. A majority of people may not have access to individual training or psychic classes or even live in a community that offers or supports such practices. Therefore, online courses supply the opportunity for someone to learn and develop their skills. Some people may fear ridicule for being openly associated with such a community and are not ready to come out of the psychic closet. I, too, began with an online course that was affordable and whose content and structure resonated with me.

There are, however, noncredible sources that are simply invested in fraud and financial gain. How do you know which are real and which are scams?

First, research the teacher. Learn their intentions and why they do the work they do. Explore their past experience, expertise, and clientele. Research how long they have been in this line of work. What are their goals? Compare the content of the course with other online courses to see if something is off or amiss with its structure and content. Determine whether the price is outrageous. If someone is offering an introductory course for an exorbitant price, run the other way. Last, determine if this course and instructor resonate with you in your gut. Intuitively you will know if this is the course for you. If you're still unsure, pray and ask for a sign and you will be shown.

A Note on Abusing Gifts

Our abilities are gifts from the creator force to be used in service to others and to help us further our own spiritual growth. We must assume great responsibility for our gifts and their power. When we act as spiritual guides, counselors, clairvoyants, and channelers, we have the power to guide others on their path in life and even, in some instances, change the direction of someone's path if they heed the message provided by spirit. Therefore, it is essential that our intentions as light workers are clear, helpful, loving, and harmless. The golden rule applies to this as well. If we help and heal others, we too will receive in like and kind, but if our intentions are harmful, deceitful, misleading, and rooted in financial gain and fame, then the same universal laws apply, and we will reap what we sow. Furthermore, please remember to express gratitude for your abilities, since this energy attracts even more blessings and creates an atmosphere that allows for the continual expansion of your gifts.

Dos and Don'ts

Do not use mind-altering drugs when meditating, channeling, and attempting to contact your spirit guides, angels, and archangels. While some cultures utilize mind-altering drugs as a way to connect or enhance their connection to the spirit world, it is not necessary and can be unpredictable and dangerous. When you have opened yourself up to channel and communicate, you are susceptible to engaging with Earthbound spirits and otherworldly beings who may not be in alignment with your higher self or have good intentions.

Do not drink alcohol when meditating, channeling, and attempting to contact your spirit guides, angels, and archangels. My guides and angels have emphasized the dangers of being intoxicated while channeling and working with the spirit world. Again, when you have opened yourself up to channel and communicate, you are susceptible to engaging with Earthbound spirits and otherworldly beings who may not be in alignment with your higher self or have good intentions.

Do not share your experiences with non-like-minded individuals at the beginning of the journey. The reason for this is that they will not encourage or support your decisions and experiences, thus planting the seed of doubt in your mind and in your journey.

Do protect yourself at all times with an appropriate protective shield.

Do meditate every day.

Conclusion

It is my hope that the information provided in this book will give you the courage and support necessary to explore beyond the boundaries of your faith. My overarching intention is to bring to light psychic and Christian principles about our identity, demonstrating that they are not diametrically opposed but instead support and equally affirm eternal spiritual truths. In alignment with biblical scripture, the psychic ministry proposes that we are made in the image of God, meaning that we are equally divine spirits, are eternally connected to God, and possess spiritual gifts as part of our divine birthright. It is my goal that with this spiritual knowledge you feel empowered, safe, and brave to awaken your psychic self.

I imagine that to some Christians, some of the exercises in this book may seem foreign or reminiscent of practices deemed oppositional to biblical scripture. In some Christian circles, the concept of meditation and going within have been demonized and defined as the trickery and deception of the Devil. However, the psychic ministry states that we are spiritually gifted, and throughout this book I have identified psychics in the Bible who were directed by God to close their eyes to witness and accept clairvoyant messages. These exercises here, all of which include meditation, help you identify, witness, and apply your gift to be of holy service. If you have been called to read this book, then know it is your intuition and a calling from above for you to awaken, trust, and grow. Thank you for investing your time and energy to open your mind to the information presented in this book. It has been a privilege to share my journey and be a part of yours.

Endnotes

Chapter One: Christian Beginnings

1. David Barton and John Cotton, *New England Primer* (1777; Aledo, TX: Wallbuilder, 1991).

Chapter Four: Communication

1. Meg Blackburn Losey, *Pyramids of Light: Awakening to Multi-dimensional Realities,* Kindle ed. (Cheney, WA: Spirit Light Resources, 2004), 57.
2. Ibid.
3. Ibid.
4. Losey, *Pyramids of Light*, 58.
5. Ibid.
6. Sonia Choquette, *The Psychic Pathway* (New York: Three Rivers, 1995).
7. Choquette, *Psychic Pathway*, 7.
8. J. Hampton Keathley III, "The Major Prophets: The Prophets of Israel Viewed as a Whole." Last modified February 21, 2016, accessed December 18, 2016, https://bible.org/seriespage/6-major-prophets
9. Ibid.
10. Jer. 1:11–14, King James Version (KJV).
11. 2 Chron. 13:22, KJV.
12. 1 Chron. 21:9, 1 & 2 Sam., KJV.
13. 1 Sam. 24:11, KJV.
14. 2 Kings 22:13–20, KJV.
15. 2 Chron. 34:22–28, KJV.
16. 1 Sam. 3:2–20, KJV.
17. 1 Chron. 9:22, KJV.
18. 2 Kings 17:13, KJV.
19. Isa. 6:1–7, KJV.
20. Isa. 6:8–13, KJV.
21. Choquette, *Psychic Pathway*, 229.
22. Ibid.
23. Choquette, *Psychic Pathway*, 187.
24. Ibid.
25. Ps. 91:11, KJV.
26. Heb. 1:14, KJV.
27. Choquette, *Psychic Pathway*, 187–189.
28. Sonia Choquette, *Ask Your Guides: Connecting to Your Divine Support System* (Carlsbad, CA: Hay House, 2006).
29. Choquette, *Psychic Pathway*, 59.
30. Ibid.
31. Ibid., 221.
32. Ibid.
33. Sanaya Roman and Duane Packer, *Opening to Channel: How to Connect with Your Guide* (Tiburon, CA: H. J. Kramer, 1984), 25–30.
34. Roman and Packer, *Opening to Channel*, 25–30.
35. Ibid.
36. Sonia Choquette, "Ask Your Guides— Information." Filmed November 14, 2012, YouTube video, 2:09, posted November 2012, www.youtube.com/watch?v=yOOxdxIuyRw.
37. Ibid.
38. Lev. 19:31, KJV.
39. Melanie Beckler, "8 Common Ascension Symptoms: Are You Actually Experiencing Ascension Symptoms?" Ask-Angels, accessed February 2, 2016,

www.ask-angels.com/spiritual-guidance/
ascension-symptoms/.

40. Natalie Wolchover, "What's So Special about the Date 11/11/11?" Last modified 2011, accessed 2015, www.livescience. com/16908-meaning-date-11-11-11. html.

41. Ibid.

42. Doreen Virtue, *Angel Numbers 101: The Meaning of 111, 123, 444, and Other Number Sequences* (Carlsbad, CA: Hay House, 2008).

Chapter Five: Life after Death

1. Gal. 5:19–21, Rev. 21:8, KJV.

2. Dan. 12:2, KJV.

3. Job. 7:21, KJV.

4. Isa. 26:19, KJV.

5. 1 Cor. 15:35–52, KJV.

6. Eccles. 12:7, KJV.

7. Gen. 2:7, KJV.

8. Job 30:19, KJV.

9. Eccles. 12:6, KJV.

10. Ps. 23:4, KJV.

11. 1 John. 14:2, KJV.

12. 2 Cor. 5:8, KJV.

13. Luke 23:43, KJV.

14. 1 Cor. 2:9, KJV.

15. Eph. 2:9, KJV.

16. Rev. 21:8, KJV.

17. Mark 9:43, KJV.

18. Mark 9:48–49, KJV.

19. Matt. 5:22, KJV.

20. Betty J. Eadie, *The Ripple Effect: Our Harvest* (Seattle, WA: Onjinjinkta, 1999).

21. Matt. 13:42, KJV.

22. John 5:28–29, KJV.

23. Rom. 2:6, KJV.

24. Rev. 20:11–12, KJV.

25. Rev. 20:13–14, KJV.

26. Matt. 25:46, KJV.

27. Rev. 1:1, KJV.

28. Rev. 20:4–6, KJV.

29. Isa. 65:17, KJV.

30. Rev. 13:1–8, KJV.

31. John 5:28–29, KJV.

32. Betty J. Eadie, *Embraced by the Light* (New York: Bantam, 1994), 29.

33. "Edgar Cayce's Near-Death Experiences: The Silver Cord and the Near-Death Experience," accessed December 2016, www.near-death.com/science/research/ silver-cord.html.

34. Ibid.

35. Raymond A. Moody Jr., *Life after Life*, 4th ed. (New York: HarperOne, 2015).

36. Eadie, *Embraced*, 42.

37. George Ritchie, *Return from Tomorrow* (Grand Rapids, MI: Revell, 1996).

38. Ibid., 37–38.

39. Ritchie, *Return*.

40. Sylvia Browne and Lindsay Harrison, *Life on the Other Side: A Psychic's Tour of the Afterlife* (New York: New American Library, 2000).

41. Ritchie, *Return*, 52.

42. Betty J. Eadie, *The Ripple Effect*.

43. Dannion Brinkley, *Saved by the Light: The True Story of a Man Who Died Twice and the Profound Revelations He Received* (New York: HarperOne, 2008), 8–83.

44. Ibid.

45. Ritchie, *Return*, 63.

46. Ibid., 64.

47. Ibid., 65–67.

48. Ibid., 59.

49. Ibid., 60.

50. Ibid.

51. Eadie, *Embraced*, 84.

52. Eadie, *Embraced*, 84–85.

53. Helen Greaves, *Testimony of Light: An Extraordinary Message of Life after Death*, Tarcher ed. (New York: Jeremy T. Tarcher / Penguin, 2009).

54. Ibid.

55. Eadie, *Embraced*, 82–85.

56. Moody, *Life after Life*, 48.

57. Michael Newton, *Journey of Souls: Case Studies of Life between Lives*, 5th rev. ed. (St. Paul, MN: Llewellyn, 2004).

58. Ibid., 34.
59. Greaves, *Testimony of Light*, 11.
60. Ibid., 19.
61. Ibid., 20.
62. Ibid.
63. Newton, *Journey of Souls*, 55.
64. Ibid., 55.
65. 1 Cor. 15:50, KJV.
66. Wyatt North, *The Life and Prayers of Saint Teresa of Avila* (Boston: Wyatt North, 2013).

Chapter Six: Lessons from Beyond the Veil
1. Rhonda Byrne, *The Secret* (New York: Atria Books, 2006).

Chapter Seven: Endings and Beginnings
1. Sanaya Roman and Duane Packer, *Opening to Channel: How to Connect with Your Guide* (Tiburon, CA: H. J. Kramer, 1984), 25–30.

Chapter Eight: Psychic Hurdles
1. Doreen Virtue, *Angel Numbers 101*.

Chapter Nine: Christianity Revisited: The Bible, Jesus, and Psychic Development
1. Matt 5:44, KJV.
2. Luke 6:27–30, KJV.
3. Matt. 22:35, Mark 12:29–31, KJV.
4. John 15:12, 17, KJV.
5. Matt. 5:8, KJV.
6. Matt. 7:12, KJV.
7. Mark 4:3–8, Matt. 13:3–8, Luke 8:5–8, KJV.
8. Prov. 4:23, KJV.
9. Matt. 4:4, KJV.
10. Matt. 9:19–22, KJV.
11. Mark 10:51–52, KJV.
12. Matt. 17:19–20, KJV.
13. Matt. 7:24–27, KJV.
14. Matt. 6:14–15, KJV.
15. John 8:7, KJV.
16. Matt. 5:14–17, KJV.
17. Rom. 8:38–39, KJV.
18. 1 Cor. 12:12–31, KJV.
19. 1 Cor. 12:1–11, KJV.
20. Matt. 26:37–38, KJV.

Chapter Ten: Spiritual Growth
1. Mark. 4:11, KJV.
2. Merriam-Webster Online, s.v. "Faith," accessed October 10, 2016, www.merriam-webster/dictionary/faith.
3. Rom. 10:17, KJV.
4. 1 Kings 19:12, KJV.
5. Heb. 11:11, KJV.

Chapter Eleven: The Basics
1. Alma Daniel, Timothy Wyllie, Andrew Ramer, *Ask Your Angels: A Practical Guide to Working with the Messengers of Heaven to Empower and Enrich Your Life* (New York: Random House, 1992).

Chapter Twelve: The Chakra System
1. Caroline Myss, *Anatomy of Spirit: The Seven Stages of Power and Healing* (New York: Crown, 1996), 68.
2. Anodea Judith, *The Wheels of Life: A User's Guide to the Chakra System* (St. Paul: Llewellyn, 1987).
3. Ibid., 24.
4. Myss, *Anatomy of Spirit*, 68.
5. Kalashatra Govinda, *A Handbook of Chakra Healing: Spiritual Practice for Health, Harmony and Inner Peace* (Old Saybrook, CT: Konecky & Konecky, 2004).
6. Ibid.
7. Judith, *Wheels of Life*, 150.
8. Govinda, *Handbook of Chakra Healing*, 29.
9. Ibid.
10. Myss, *Anatomy of Spirit*, 99.
11. Ibid., 100.
12. Matt. 6:9–13, KJV.

Chapter Fourteen: Connecting with Spirit Guides and Angels

1. Sonia Choquette, "Ask Your Guides—Information," filmed November 14, 2012, YouTube Video, 2:09, www.youtube.com/watch?v=yOOxdxluyRw.
2. Ps. 91:11–12, KJV.
3. Doreen Virtue, *Angel Numbers 101*.
4. Daniel, Wyllie, and Ramer, *Ask Your Angels*.
5. Gustav Davidson, *A Dictionary of Angels: Including the Fallen Angels* (New York: Free Press, 1994).
6. Ibid.
7. Rosemary Ellen Guiley, *Encyclopedia of Angels* (New York: Facts on File, 1996).

Chapter Fifteen: Tools and Exercises for Psychic Expansion

1. Losey, *Pyramids of Light*.
2. Donald Tyson, *Scrying for Beginners* (St. Paul, MN: Llewellyn, 1997).
3. Rosemary Ellen Guiley, *The Art of Black Mirror Scrying* (New Milford, CT: Visionary Living, 2014).

Bibliography

Barton, David, and John Cotton, *New England Primer*. 1777. Aledo, TX: Wallbuilder, 1991.

Beckler, Melanie. "8 Common Ascension Symptoms: Are You Actually Experiencing Ascension Symptoms?" Accessed February 2, 2016, www.ask-angels.com/spiritual-guidance/ascension-symptoms/.

Brinkley, Dannion. *Saved by the Light: The True Story of a Man Who Died Twice and the Profound Revelations He Received*. New York: HarperOne, 2008 (originally published in 1994).

Browne, Sylvia, and Lindsay Harrison. *Life on the Other Side: A Psychic's Tour of the Afterlife*. New York: New American Library, 2000.

Byrne, Rhonda. *The Secret*. New York: Atria Books, 2006.

Choquette, Sonia. *Ask Your Guides: Connecting to Your Divine Support System*. Carlsbad, CA: Hay House, 2006.

———. *The Psychic Pathway*. New York: Three Rivers, 1995.

Daniel, Alma, Timothy Wyllie, and Andrew Ramer. *Ask Your Angels: A Practical Guide to Working with the Messengers of Heaven to Empower and Enrich Your Life*. New York: Random House, 1992.

Davidson, Gustav. *A Dictionary of Angels: Including the Fallen Angels*. New York: Free Press, 1994.

Eadie, Betty J. *Embraced by the Light*. New York: Bantam, 1994.

———. *The Ripple Effect: Our Harvest*. Seattle, WA: Onjinjinkta, 1999.

"Edgar Cayce's Near-Death Experiences: The Silver Cord and the Near-Death Experience." Accessed December 2016, www.near-death.com/science/research/silver-cord.html.

Govinda, Kalashatra. *A Handbook of Chakra Healing: Spiritual Practice for Health, Harmony and Inner Peace*. Old Saybrook, CT: Konecky & Konecky, 2004.

Greaves, Helen. *Testimony of Light: An Extraordinary Message of Life after Death*. New York: Jeremy T. Tarcher / Penguin, 2009, Tarcher edition (originally published in 1969).

Guiley, Rosemary Ellen. *Encyclopedia of Angels*. New York: Facts on File, 1996.

———. *The Art of Black Mirror Scrying*. New Milford, CT: Visionary Living, 2014.

Johnson, Ken. *Ancient Book of Enoch*. Charleston, SC: CreateSpace, 2012.

Judith, Anodea. *Wheels of Life: A User's Guide to the Chakra System*. St. Paul, MN: Llewellyn, 1987.

Keathley, J. Hampton, III. "The Major Prophets: The Prophets of Israel Viewed as a Whole." Last modified February 21, 2016, accessed December 18, 2016, https://bible.org/seriespage/6-major-prophets.

Losey, Meg Blackburn. *Pyramids of Light: Awakening to Multi-dimensional Realities*. Cheney, WA: Spirit Light Resources, 2004. Kindle edition.

Moody, Raymond A., Jr. *Life after Life*. 4th ed. New York: HarperOne, 2015.

Myss, Caroline. *Anatomy of the Spirit: The Seven Stages of Power and Healing*. New York: Crown, 1996.

Newton, Michael. *Journey of Souls: Case Studies of Life between Lives*. 5th rev. ed. St. Paul, MN: Llewellyn, 2004 (originally published in 1994).

North, Wyatt. *The Life and Prayers of Saint Teresa of Avila*. Boston: Wyatt North, 2013.

O'Neill, Jennifer. *Keys to the Spirit World: An Easy to Use Handbook for Contacting Your Spirit Guides*. Jennifer O'Neill, 2012. Kindle edition.

Ritchie, George. *Return from Tomorrow*. Grand Rapids, MI: Revell, 1996.

Roman, Sanaya, and Duane Packer. *Opening to Channel: How to Connect with Your Guide*. Tiburon, CA: H. J. Kramer, 1984.

Tyson, Donald. *Scrying for Beginners*. St. Paul, MN: Llewellyn, 1997.

Virtue, Doreen. *Angel Numbers 101: The Meaning of 111, 123, 444, and Other Number Sequences*. Carlsbad, CA: Hay House, 2008.

Wolchover, Natalie. "What's So Special about the Date 11/11/11?" Last modified 2011, accessed 2015, www.livescience.com/16908-meaning-date-11-11-11.html.

Other Schiffer Books on Related Subjects

THE PSYCHIC WORKBOOK
Tools and Techniques to
Develop Reliable Insight.
Karen Fox, PhD

THE PSALM® CARDS
and Messages from the Psalms.
Rabbi Robert dos Santos Teixeira,
LCSW

ISBN: 978-0-7643-4816-7

ISBN: 978-0-7643-5191-4